What is the Baha'i Faith?

What is the Baha'i Faith?

by

William McElwee Miller

An Abridgment by

William N. Wysham

William B. Eerdmans Publishing Company

This book is an abridgment of *The Baha'i
Faith: Its History and Teachings,* by
William McElwee Miller, Copyright © 1974
by *William Carey Library,* 533 Hermosa Street,
South Pasadena, Calif. 91030

Library of Congress Cataloging in Publication Data

Miller, William McElwee.
     What is the Baha'i faith?

     Abridgment of The Bahai faith.
     1. Bahaism.   1. Wysham, William N.   II. Title.
BP365.M49 1977 297'.89 77-8063
ISBN 0-8028-1701-1

Contents

Preface 7

Introduction 9

1. The Islamic Background 11
2. The Manifestation of the Bab 15
3. The Doctrines and Decrees of the Bab 22
4. The Vicegerency of Subh-i-Azal 32
5. The Schism Between Two Brothers 43
6. The Manifestation of Baha'u'llah 48
7. The Doctrines and Decrees of Baha'u'llah 56
8. The Rule of Abdu'l-Baha 69
9. The Baha'i Faith Goes West and East 78
10. The Teachings of Abdu'l-Baha 90
11. The Guardianship of Shoghi Effendi 106
12. The Rule of the People 125
13. Conclusion 143

Preface

THERE WAS A TIME not long ago when Eastern religions were found largely in the East, and people in the West had little knowledge of or interest in them. That is not the case today. Large numbers of young people and others in the West are showing intense interest in some of the religious movements that have come from the East, and many have become enthusiastic devotees of these faiths.

One of the Eastern religions now active in the West which is attracting the attention of both students and older people is the Baha'i World Faith. While not a new movement, having originated in Iran more than a century ago, and while not as aggressive as some of the newer cults, it is actively engaged in giving its message and making converts, and it claims to be *the* religion of the world for the next one thousand years.

Some who have come in touch with the Baha'i movement wish to hear not only what the followers of this Faith say, but what others think of it. To meet this need, Dr. William M. Miller, who long resided in Iran as a Christian missionary, wrote a definitive appraisal entitled *The Baha'i Faith: Its History and Teachings,* which was published in 1974 by William Carey Library, 533 Hermosa Street, South Pasadena, Cal. 91030; price $8.95 (postage paid). This volume is available for those who wish to make a thorough study of the Baha'i movement.

Now, to provide readers with the essential material of the larger volume, without the lengthy quotations and numerous footnotes which fill 443 pages, a briefer and less expensive edition is called for. The present volume, all the contents of which (excepting the necessary summaries and connecting passages) are found in Dr. Miller's longer book, has been prepared to meet this need. All readers of this condensation can be assured that full documentation for every historical statement and the sources of all quotations are available in the larger volume in the form of copious notes and references. It is hoped that many who read this abridged edition will also wish to own the larger book, which contains the full text in English of the Arabic *Kitab-i-Aqdas* (Most Holy Book), the basic Baha'i scripture.

Because Dr. Miller's account of the Babi-Baha'i movement differs radically in many respects from that related in the Baha'i publications, his book has been criticized by Baha'i leaders, and members of the Faith have been advised not to read it. However, all who wish to understand this movement should read both the Baha'i literature and Dr. Miller's scholarly and authoritative treatment of the history and teachings of Baha'ism. Since advocates of this "World Faith" make use of every opportunity, through the press and radio, by invitations to group meetings in many communities, and especially in academic circles, to promote Baha'ism as a world religion and the successor to all others, including Christianity, students and other seekers for truth should consider carefully the Baha'i claims in the light of the material provided by a Christian writer well acquainted with this Faith.

It has been a privilege for me to prepare this condensation, which I consider a valid appraisal of the Baha'i claims.

WILLIAM N. WYSHAM

Introduction

WHEN A YOUNG MAN named Ali Muhammad, who lived in the city of Shiraz in Persia,* announced in 1844 A.D. that he had a divine mission, who would have dreamed that one day this would result in a golden-domed Shrine to him in Haifa, Palestine, to be visited by thousands of pilgrims from many lands? And who could have predicted that Ali Muhammad was destined to initiate a movement which would spread to all parts of the earth? Perhaps the young prophet himself envisioned a glorious future for his cause, but not many of his countrymen, and no one outside of Persia, shared his dreams. Yet Ali Muhammad, better known as the Bab, is now revered by all who profess allegiance to the "Baha'i World Faith."

This movement, which began when Ali Muhammad announced that he was the Bab (Gate), was continued and developed by another man from Persia first known as Baha, and later as Baha'u'llah. The followers of this Faith, known as Baha'is, maintain that it is the true religion for this age for all the people of the world, and that it will unite all races and religions in one happy family. It is the purpose of this book to trace the development of Baha'ism and acquaint the reader with its teachings.

WILLIAM McELWEE MILLER

*Now known as Iran (Ee-ráhn), the name its people have always called their country.

1

The Islamic Background

IT IS AS IMPOSSIBLE for one to understand the Baha'i
Faith without a knowledge of Islam as it would be to
understand Christianity without a knowledge of the Old
Testament. The Baha'i religion is an offshoot of Shi'ite
Islam, and though modern Baha'is may emphasize the
universal aspects of their faith and strive to disassociate
themselves from the past, the foundations of their system
rest on the soil of Iran, and are saturated with Islamic
conceptions. It is impossible to give here a full account of
the rise of Islam and the development of the doctrines,
practices, and civilization of the Muslims, and the reader
is referred to the excellent books on Islam which are now
available. We include only a brief account of the historical background of the Babi movement. *Achmed*

In the year 570 A.D. there was born in the city of
Mecca in Arabia a baby named ~~Muhammad,~~ who was
destined to change the religion, politics, and culture of
a large part of the world. Living among people who
worshipped idols, but who knew of a Supreme Deity
whom they called Allah (The God), Muhammad became
acquainted with Jews and Christians who did not worship images. It was probably, in part at least, a result
of his contacts with them that Muhammad, at forty years
of age, developed a strong conviction that Allah had appointed him to be a prophet, and thereafter Muhammad
was sure that revelations from Allah were brought to

11

him from Heaven by the angel Gabriel. These divine
messages were spoken by Muhammad, were written
down by those who heard them (it is generally supposed
that Muhammad was illiterate), and were later collected
in a book called the Qur'an (Koran). By his preaching,
and later by the use of the sword, Muhammad was able
to make himself the religious and also the political ruler
of most of Arabia.

Muhammad made no definite provision for a successor, one to which all of his followers agreed. On his
death in 632 A.D. the majority of his believers united in
choosing Abu Bakr as Caliph (meaning "vicar" or "successor"), and he ruled the church-state of Islam in
Muhammad's place. Abu Bakr was succeeded in turn by
'Umar, 'Uthman, and Ali; these four were known as the
Rightly-Guided Caliphs, and were all chosen in the same
manner. The last three were assassinated by other Muslims. To the democratic Arabs it seemed altogether
proper that their chief should be appointed by the people; they held that the voice of the people was the voice
of God. It was during the reigns of the first four Caliphs
that the armies of the Arabs poured forth from their
barren deserts, overthrew the forces of Persia and Byzantium, and conquered Mesopotamia, Syria, the Iranian
plateau, and Egypt for Islam. It was their belief that
Muslims must rule the whole world.

However, there soon developed in Islam a party
whose members held a theory of the succession totally
different from that held by the ruling party. To them it
seemed as impossible for the successor of the Prophet
to be elected by the people as it would have been for
the Prophet himself to be thus chosen. They contended
that as a Prophet must be chosen by God, not by the
people, so must the Prophet's successor be appointed by
God and named specifically by the Prophet. This party
was called "Shi'ite" (meaning "separatist"). Though
there came to be many divisions among Shi'ites, all held

firmly to the principle that the successor of Muhammad, whom they called not Caliph but "Imam" (meaning "leader"), must be a descendant of the Prophet, and must be nominated explicitly by his predecessor. The supreme duty of the believer was to recognize and yield allegiance to the rightful Imam.

The Shi'ites held that Ali, the cousin and son-in-law of Muhammad (Muhammad left no son to be his heir) was the first Imam, or vice-regent of their Prophet. Thus, from early times, the Muslim world was divided between the Shi'ites and their opponents, the Sunnites, and this division has remained until the present day. The people of Iran were especially susceptible to Shi'ite influences. They generally despised the Arabs by whom they had been conquered, and in espousing the cause of Ali and his descendants they found an opportunity to express their national spirit and maintain something of their independence. The Iranians, unlike the democratic Arabs, were imbued with the doctrine of the divine right of kings, and had even considered their rulers to be divine beings. They were therefore quite ready, after their defeat by the Arabs, to give the Imams the place in their affection which their own kings had previously occupied, and to look upon them as supernatural beings, free from all sin and imperfection, and endowed with miraculous powers, who ought by divine right to rule over them in both temporal and spiritual affairs. It is estimated that ninety-eight per cent of the people of Iran are Muslims, the great majority of whom belong to that sect of the Shi'ites which acknowledges twelve Imams. Its followers affirm that Ali and ten of the descendants who succeeded him suffered violent deaths at the hands of the Sunnites, and are counted as holy martyrs. They believe, however, that the twelfth Imam, Muhammad son of Hasan al-Askari, who disappeared during childhood immediately following the death of his father in 873 A.D., is still alive and will again appear on earth. "For in every age," they say, "there must be an Imam immune to sin."

Among the Shi'ites there have been various sects whose members have not contented themselves with considering the Prophets and Imams to be supernatural and sinless beings with miraculous powers, but have exalted them yet more highly, regarding them as emanations of Deity and Manifestations of God. These sects have been rejected by the Twelvers as heretical, but from time to time in the history of Iran we find individuals putting forward the claim that they are the "return" of some previous prophet or Imam, and are Divine Manifestations.

One of the more recent heretical sects to appear in Iran — a sect rejected and hated by the Twelvers — was that of the Shaykhis, the followers of Shaykh Ahmad al-Ahsa'i, who died in 1826. He taught that the twelve Imams were divine beings, that there must always be on earth a person who is in direct contact with the Hidden Imam, and that the Resurrection is spiritual, not physical. During his lifetime he was considered by his disciples to be the channel of grace between believers and the Hidden Imam, as was also his successor Sayyid Kazim of Resht. Both of these men were sometimes given the title "Bab" (Gate). These Shaykhi teachers led their disciples to expect the appearance of the Hidden Imam himself in the near future. Some traditions said that he would return after a thousand years, and, according to the Muslim calendar, the time was at hand. Thus Shi'ites of all sects were impatiently awaiting his manifestation.

When Sayyid Kazim died in 1843, his disciples were for some time in doubt as to whom they should turn for guidance. Soon two rival claimants for the leadership appeared, and the Shaykhi brotherhood was torn between them. One faction followed Hajji Karim Khan of Kirman, and continued to go by the name "Shaykhi." The other faction, which was the stronger, followed Sayyid Ali Muhammad of Shiraz, who adopted the title "Bab." Hence, his followers became known as Babis.

2

The Manifestation of the Bab

SAYYID ALI MUHAMMAD, better known to the world as
the Bab, was born in Shiraz in the province of Pars in
the southern part of Iran in 1820 (or possibly 1819). He
was a descendant of the family of Muhammad the
Prophet of Islam. His father, a cloth merchant in Shiraz,
died when his son was quite young, and the child was
left to the care of his maternal uncle, Hajji Mirza Ali,
who raised him. It is said that he was quiet and modest,
and that as he grew older he became studious and pious.
When he was about seventeen years of age he was sent
to Bushire, the port on the Persian Gulf, to help with
his uncle's business. There he earned his living by trade,
and spent his spare time in his studies.

After several years the young man, disinclined to
continue his commercial pursuits, and becoming increasingly interested in matters of religion, left Bushire for
Shiraz. After a short stay there he made a pilgrimage
to the shrines of the Shi'ite Imams near Baghdad in
Iraq, and remained for perhaps a year. While in Karbala, the site of the tomb of the Imam Husayn, grandson
of Muhammad, who was martyred there in 680 A.D.,
Sayyid Ali Muhammad became acquainted with Hajji

Sayyid Kazim of Resht, the head of the Shaykhi movement, and was profoundly influenced by Kazim's lectures, which he attended eagerly. He, in turn, by his
gentleness and devotion, won the esteem and affection
of his teacher and fellow students. From Karbala, Sayyid
Ali Muhammad returned to Shiraz, and was married
there in 1842.

It is not possible to trace in detail the changes that
took place in the mind and heart of Sayyid Ali Muhammad during these years. He had probably become dis-
gusted by what he had seen and experienced of Islam
as it was then practiced in Iran and Iraq. The lectures
of Hajji Sayyid Kazim had centered his attention on the
Imams, no doubt particularly on the Hidden Imam who
would surely come soon as the long-expected Mahdi and
right the wrongs of the world. Long meditation and much
prayer brought to Sayyid Ali Muhammad the conviction
that he himself had been chosen by God for a special
mission to men. Accordingly, in his native city of Shiraz,
on May 23, 1844, when he was twenty-four, he made the
historic declaration which marked the beginning of the
Babi-Baha'i movement.

The first person to hear and attest the claim of the
Bab was Mulla Muhammad Husayn of Bushruieh, a
small town in eastern Iran. Mulla Husayn was a man of
learning, influence, and great force of character. He had
been one of the followers of Hajji Sayyid Kazim, and
in Karbala had become acquainted with the young student from Shiraz. About five months after the death of
his master he came to Shiraz and called upon his fellow
student. To his great surprise, Sayyid Ali Muhammad
quietly informed him of his mission and by reading to
him portions of his writings and answering questions
about difficult points of theology, convinced his guest
that he was the possessor of supernatural knowledge.

After several days of doubt and indecision, Mulla
Husayn enthusiastically professed faith in the Bab, who

conferred on him the title "Babu'l-Bab" (Gate of the Gate). Gradually others believed, till there were eighteen disciples. The last of these was Mulla Muhammad Ali of Barfurush, a city near the Caspian Sea, to whom the Bab gave the title "Quddus" (Holy). These eighteen were called by the Bab "Letters of the Living."

The new disciples, who became known as "Babis," went forth to other cities and began to proclaim with great boldness and zeal the advent of the Bab. Some who heard the news thought he must be the return of the Hidden Imam. Although Sayyid Ali Muhammad had not yet proclaimed in full the nature of his mission, it seems that the Letters of the Living understood clearly that he claimed to bring a new revelation, to be a new Manifestation of God. They read to the people the writings which the Bab had composed, and pointed to them as a proof of his divine mission, just as Muslims have always pointed to the verses of the Koran as the all-sufficient proof of the mission of Muhammad. Thus, a great stir began to occur all over Iran, some people showing great eagerness to believe the good news, and others treating the Bab's apostles with disrespect and even blows.

While his followers were thus engaged, the Bab and one of the Letters set out near the end of 1844 for Mecca, where, according to one tradition, the Mahdi would make his appearance. There the Bab proclaimed himself to a few of the pilgrims. It is said that he also addressed an Epistle, in which he declared his mission, to the Sharif of Mecca, who ignored it. Then he started back toward Shiraz, and early in the year 1845 reached Bushire. While he tarried there, one of his zealous disciples, Mulla Sadiq by name, in giving the call to prayer in a mosque in Shiraz, openly added the formula, "I testify that Ali Muhammad is the Gate of God." This innovation incensed many people, and several of the Babis who were held responsible for it were, at the order of the governor, seized, severely beaten, and expelled from the city.

Horsemen were sent to Bushire to arrest the Bab and bring him to Shiraz. After his arrival in September, 1845, he was examined by the governor, who, fearing further trouble, kept him under observation.

To understand the attitude of the government officials toward Sayyid Ali Muhammad and the movement which his claim had inspired, it is necessary to remember that in the history of Islam, putting forward a claim to be the Hidden Imam has always been connected with a political uprising. In arresting the Bab the authorities were only doing their duty, attempting to forestall a probable upheaval. But this attempt proved unsuccessful; the fire had already been kindled, and was spreading rapidly throughout the land. The people had long expected a deliverer. The government of the country was corrupt and inefficient. The popular religion was full of superstition, and had failed to bring moral and spiritual renewal to the people of Iran. The Muslim clergy were often both ignorant and evil men. The rich oppressed the poor, whose lot was pitiable. The time was indeed ripe for a revolution. And now, just one thousand years after the disappearance of the Twelfth Imam, the rightful ruler who at his return would bring in the new order, the cry was raised far and near that the Lord of the Age had come! Bold and eloquent apostles proclaimed his advent all through Iran, and multitudes were eager to believe on him. It is not surprising that the government became alarmed, and took drastic measures to nip the movement in the bud.

Some time after the Bab's arrival in Shiraz, the religious authorities also became greatly disturbed at the course of events. It is said that they brought pressure on the maternal uncle of the Bab to force his nephew to make a formal denial of his claims. The Bab, accordingly, went to one of the mosques in Shiraz, and to the great joy of the clergy read a statement which they took to be a complete denial. However, at a later time the Bab

explained in writing that he meant in his denial of Bab-
hood that he was not a Bab *in the traditional Shi'ite
sense of the term,* and that he did not claim to be a Gate
to the knowledge of the Hidden Imam. Later he made it
clear that his claim was to be a Gate of God, that is, a
Major Manifestation.

During the next few years the Bab and his teachings
continued to create a great furor in Iran. He was at first
befriended by the governor of Isfahan where he had
gone, but the governor's successor, wishing to show his
loyalty to the Shah, put him on the road to Teheran, the
capital, under escort. Before he arrived, the Shah sent
him to Maku, a fortress on the northern frontier, five
hundred miles away. On the journey and while many
months a prisoner at Maku, the Bab conducted himself
with great mildness and patience. He was treated kindly
and many of his followers came from a distance to visit
him. He was then transferred to a castle near Lake
Urumia (now Rezaieh) where he remained for more
than two years.

During this imprisonment the Bab was summoned to
Tabriz by the Crown Prince, then governor of the area,
and was examined concerning his claims. The mullas
(Muslim clergy) who questioned him were completely
hostile, made no serious effort to understand his claims,
and had him bastinadoed afterwards. He was returned
to prison to await the decision of the government in
Teheran. He remained there till his execution, engaged
in writing his books and epistles, setting forth his claims,
and making laws for his Theocratic Society.

While the Bab was in prison in Maku and later in
Chihriq, his fiery missionaries travelled busily about
Iran calling upon the Shi'ites to accept him as their long-
expected Mahdi. Toward the end of the year 1847 Mulla
Husayn of Bushruieh, the First Letter of the Living,
went eastward to the province of Khurasan, meeting
great success everywhere. In Nishapur, the city of Omar

Khayyam, several members of the Muslim clergy believed, and it seemed for a time that the whole city might follow their example. But when he reached Meshed, the shrine city of the Imam Reza, the eighth in succession after Muhammad, whose tomb is visited annually by hundreds of thousands of Shi'ite pilgrims, the mullas rose against him and had him arrested. However, he managed to escape, and seeing that he was in peril he gathered a number of his converts about him and proceeded westward in the direction of Teheran. Others joined him along the way, and his band became quite formidable. Before long a fight occurred with the Muslims, the Babis were worsted, and they fell back on Shahrud, later proceeding toward the northern province of Mazanderan.

In the meantime a number of Babi leaders had gathered in a place called Badasht near Shahrud. Here, in the spring of 1848, while the Bab was still in Maku, a conference of the Babi chiefs was held. At this gathering the abrogation of the laws of the previous Islamic dispensation was announced, thus indicating that these Babis considered the Bab to be, not the Twelfth Imam who had returned, but a new Prophet in place of Muhammad. It was at Badasht that Mirza Husayn Ali, one of the zealous Babis, received the title "Baha" (Splendor). It was not bestowed by the Bab, the sole grantor of titles.

The Babis next moved into Mazanderan with the full intention of getting control of that province. The time was propitious, for in September, 1848, Muhammad Shah had died and the new king, Nasiru'd-Din Shah, had not yet ascended the throne, so no one was prepared to oppose their designs. More than three hundred strong, they entered Barfurush armed. Thus provoking strife, they were soon attacked by the Muslims, and several of them were killed. Then the Babis began to fight. Mulla Husayn, the first to believe on the Bab, attacked the man who had killed the first Babi and "sliced him like a fresh

cucumber." Six other Muslims were killed. One of the
Babis who was taken by the townfolk was buried alive
in a well. After a pitched battle lasting several days in
Barfurush, the Babis were allowed to retire. They went
into the forest and built themselves a fort in which it is
said two thousand Babis assembled and there defied the
government.

This and other similar incidents led the government
to send force after force into Mazanderan to restore
order. Two of these were repulsed in bloody encounters
but the royal army finally prevailed and the Babi leaders
were executed. A Muslim historian stated that five hundred of the Shah's soldiers and fifteen hundred Babis
lost their lives in these conflicts. A year later another
serious Babi uprising occurred in the city of Zenjan in
northwest Iran. The Shah sent regiment after regiment
but the Babis defended themselves with frenzied courage. The fighting dragged on for months and ended only
late in 1850 when the surviving Babis were all put to
the sword. Still other uprisings occurred in several cities
and the government decided that the Bab himself must
be got rid of, not because of his religious views but for
the good of the state. Accordingly, he was brought to
Tabriz from his prison and publicly executed there. The
night before, he urged his disciples to repudiate him and
his doctrines in order to save their lives. All but one,
Mirza Muhammad Ali, did so. He and the Bab, on July 8,
1850, were dragged through the streets to the citadel and
executed by firing squads of soldiers. After the death
of the Bab the fighting ceased.

3

The Doctrines and Decrees of the Bab

BEFORE CONTINUING the history of the Babi movement after the death of its founder, we must pause to give an account of the Bab's teachings and precepts. This is no easy task, for the writings in which the Bab expounded his doctrines were numerous, and their style is sometimes most difficult. The Bab wrote both in Persian, his mother tongue, and in Arabic, the language of the Koran, which to most of the people in Iran was a foreign and largely unknown tongue. Many of the Bab's books were not preserved by his followers, but there are a number of volumes still in existence today. These are rare, and with a few exceptions are in manuscript and have never been translated or printed.

The Bab gave distinctive names to his earlier books. However, most of his later writings were included under the term *"Bayan"* (Utterance, Exposition). The Bab himself classified all his writings under five categories: (1) Verses in the style of the Koran, (2) Prayers and supplications, (3) Commentaries, (4) Scientific treatises, and (5) Persian treatises. In the opinion of the Bab the *Bayan* has no equal, for it is incomparable and inimitable. He says that if all creatures on earth should unite, they could not produce the like of it. It is identical in essence with the Gospel and the Koran. Whoever believes in it is in Paradise. It includes all things. It must be written in the best handwriting (or may be printed), and carefully preserved. It is to be bound in nineteen volumes. The believer is to read seven hundred verses of the *Bayan* night and morning, and if he cannot do this he is to mention God seven hundred times by saying *"Allahu Azhar"* (God is Most Manifest).

In a study of the Bab's teachings one of the most important matters to be considered is his claim for himself. Among the Shi'ites there was no expectation that the Hidden Imam would give new laws to men upon his appearing, for it was assumed that the Koranic laws were God's final revelations and would never be replaced by others. But when Sayyid Ali Muhammad wanted to convince men that he had a divine mission he did just what the Prophet Muhammad had done, pointed to his verses and writings, and said that no one else could produce the like of them. He also began to issue laws and regulations for the religious, social, and civil life of men, as Muhammad had done. And his verses in Arabic imitated the Koran, with which he said his *Bayan* was identical. In his book, *Seven Proofs,* he argued that if it were a miracle, as Muslims agree it was, that Muhammad produced a small book (the Koran) in his native tongue, it was surely a greater miracle that, in a few hours, a young man from Iran should be able to write thousands of verses in Arabic, which to him was a foreign language, and produce a huge book like the *Bayan,* which surpasses the Koran in spiritual knowledge and eloquence. The Bab definitely considered himself to be, not an Imam, but a Prophet superior to Muhammad.

From his declaration in 1844 till 1848 Sayyid Ali Muhammad made himself known as the Bab. Then, while still in Maku, he proclaimed that he was the Qa'im and Mahdi. It has generally been supposed that he was using these terms in their Shi'ite sense, and that he, who had till then only claimed to be the Gate (Bab) to the Hidden Imam, at this time put forth a higher claim, namely, that he was himself the Imam, who was commonly called the Mahdi or Qa'im. However, in making this declaration the Bab adopted the title "Qa'im" (He Who Ariseth) with a new meaning, for in the *Bayan* he stated that it meant "He who prevails over all men, whose arising is the Resurrection." The *Bayan* makes it quite clear that the Bab claimed to be a major prophet. In his own eyes, as in the eyes of his followers, Sayyid Ali Muhammad inaugurated a new Prophetic Cycle, and brought a new Revelation, the *Bayan,* which abrogated the Koran, as the Koran had abrogated the Gospels.

The Bab did not imagine, however, that his would be the final Manifestation. As the Sun of Truth had risen again and again in ages past, each Manifestation more perfect than the one which preceded it, so it would continue to arise in ages to come. Hence the Bab spoke of the Prophet in the next Resurrection as "He-Whom-God-Will-Manifest." One of the striking features of the Bab's writings is the frequent reference which is made to this greater Manifestation which is to follow him. In the *Persian Bayan* alone the term He-Whom-God-Will-Manifest is found some seventy times. The People of the *Bayan,* as the followers of the Bab are called, must all accept Him, and not be like the Jews who rejected Jesus, and the Christians who rejected Muhammad, and the Muslims who have rejected him, the Bab. He-Whom-God-Will-Manifest is divine, and is one with the Point of the *Bayan* and all other Manifestations. All previous Manifestations were created for Him, and one verse revealed by Him is better than a thousand *Bayans.* If one should hear a single verse from Him, and recite it, it is better than that he should recite the *Bayan* a thousand times. He only can abrogate the *Bayan.* He will arise suddenly, and no one can claim falsely to be He. Only God knows the time of His coming, but the Bab refers to the time by the number of the words *Ghiyath* and *Mustaghath*. Each letter of the Arabic alphabet has a numerical value, and the letters of these words have the value of 1511 and 2001 respectively. It is clear, therefore, that the Bab expected the next Manifestation after 1511, and before 2001, years.

Though doctrinal discussions, mystical meditations, and countless prayers for use when visiting sacred shrines and on other occasions occupy a large place in the Bab's writings, he also gave many specific directions for the life of his followers on earth. He proposed, as Muhammad had done, to set up a universal Theocratic Society, and issued laws for the regulation of both the civil and religious affairs of the People of the *Bayan*. The Bab decreed that all their activities should be governed by groups of nineteen persons. For instance, each city and village was to have one or more temples for worship, each of which was to be in the charge of nineteen attendants. Shrines were to be erected only over the graves of the Bab and the eighteen Letters, and these nineteen Holy Places would embrace under their shadow the graves of other martyrs and holy men. The holy places of previous dispensations were no longer to be preserved. All believers living within two hundred fifty miles of the Bab's tomb must visit it every year, provided they be in good circumstances, and remain for at least ten days. Also, they must visit the tombs of the eighteen Letters, travelling on foot if possible. Pilgrims to these Holy Places must give gifts to each of the nineteen guardians in each shrine.

In addition to these pilgrimages, yet another was required, namely, that to the "Place of the Blow" in Tabriz. This was the house in which the Bab got the bastinado after his first trial. Every believer residing in Tabriz or within a radius of 412 miles of Tabriz, who reached the age of twenty-nine and was in good circumstances, was required to visit this Place every year, to remain there nineteen days, and to perform the prescribed rites. Those who are too poor to do this must perform the rites at home.

Non-Babis were not permitted to reside in the dominions of a Babi monarch, and no unbeliever was to reside in Fars, Central Iran, Khurasan, Mazanderan, or Azarbaijan, the provinces of Iran where the Babi faith had first been propagated. However, non-Babis who carried on business which benefited Babis were exempted from these prohibitions.

A Babi monarch was authorized to seize the properties of non-Babis in his dominions, but if they embraced the Babi faith their properties were to be restored. In the event of the conquest of a country by Babi armies, the most priceless property was to be reserved for the Bab, if he were alive. If he were dead, it was to be held for Him-Whom-God-Will-Manifest.

Whatever severity might be used toward unbelievers, the Bab enjoined the greatest kindness and gentleness toward brothers in the faith. He did not authorize corporal punishment or imprisonment or the use of force, and capital punishment had no place in his system of government. If taxes were not paid they were not to be forcibly collected. The only punishments appointed for the People of the *Bayan* were fines, and prohibitions for men to approach their wives, who presumably did not share their guilt. It is not clear how these punishments were to be administered.

It seems that the Bab may have wished to abolish the outward forms of religion which have played so important a part in the lives of many Muslims. This, however, would have been unacceptable to most of his followers, and so he contented himself with lightening somewhat the burden of ceremonialism.

The People of the *Bayan* were permitted to deal in business with unbelievers. Though unbelievers and their property were considered to be unclean, any property transferred by them to believers became clean "because of the honor accorded to it by reason of the association with the Babi faith."

The Muslim worship which the Shi'ites are required to perform at least three times each day in the Arabic language while facing Mecca was abolished by the Bab. There was to be no congregational worship, like that in the mosques on Friday, except for the dead. Whether in the place of worship or at home, worship was to be performed individually, so there was no need for an order of clergy to lead the worshippers. The one time of required worship was noon, when the "Unity Prayer" was to be recited. This act of worship consisted of nineteen prostrations made as the worshipper presumably faced the House of the Bab in Shiraz. The words to be spoken in Arabic nineteen times in this daily act of worship were as follows:

> God witnesseth that there is no god but He: to Him belongeth creation and command. He quickeneth and causeth to die: then He causeth to die and quickeneth, and verily He is the Living, who dieth not. In His grasp is the dominion of all things: He createth what he pleaseth by His command: verily He has power over all things.

The Muslim month of fasting, Ramazan, lasts a full lunar month, and when it falls in summer the faithful must refrain from taking food and drink for almost eighteen hours each day for twenty-eight days. The Bab reduced the Fast to one Bayanic month of nineteen days, making it last from sunrise to sunset. And since the Babi Fast always comes in the spring of the year, and is the last month of the Babi year, which immediately precedes No Ruz, the New Year Festival (March 21), in Iran it does not last longer than twelve hours. As in the Muslim Fast, eating and drinking are permitted at night.

The Bab placed great importance upon marriage, which he made obligatory upon all believers. At the age of eleven, or at latest when believers reach the age of puberty, they must marry. In the cities the man at marriage must give to the woman a minimum of nineteen and a maximum of ninety-five *mithqals* of gold, and in the rural areas the same amount in silver. A man was permitted to have two wives, but polygamy was discouraged, and the form of concubinage permitted by Shi'ite law was strictly forbidden. The Bab himself had at least two wives. Divorce was permitted after a year. If one of the parties in marriage died, the widower must remarry within ninety days, and the widow within ninety-five days. Though the Bab had no children of his own except an infant who died, he showed great concern for the training of children. He forbade the beating of boys by their masters, and all other cruel punishments. It is probable that his emphasis on kindness and love, as well as his attitude toward women and children, was influenced by his reading of the New Testament, which was translated into Persian in Shiraz by Henry Martyn nine years before the Bab was born there, and was published four years later. The use of the veil by women, according to the Muslim custom, was forbidden by the Bab, and men and women were permitted to associate with one another freely, but were enjoined to avoid all over-familiarity. The Bab had seen Christians in Isfahan and Azarbaijan, and in the *Bayan* he spoke favorably of their cleanliness and dignity, and was no doubt impressed by their customs. But he stated that in spite of all their good qualities they are still in the Fire (unbelief), because they did not accept Muhammad, who is superior to Jesus.

Since the numerical value of the Arabic word *Wáhid* (One, that is, God the One) is nineteen, the Bab thought that everything should be arranged on the basis of the number nineteen. He accordingly proposed a new calendar with nineteen months of nineteen days each (19 x 19 = 361)

> . . . that all may advance through the 19 degrees of the Letters of the Unity from the point of entrance (into the sign of) the Ram to the limit of its course . . . in the sign of the Fish.

By rejecting the Muslim lunar calendar, and making the ancient Iranian New Year (No Ruz), which usually falls on March 21, the vernal equinox, the beginning of the Babi year, it seems that the Bab wished to demonstrate his patriotic feelings.

The Bab issued many other regulations for his followers, a few of which we will mention. According to his decree, all books revealed by God in previous prophetic dispensations, presumably the Bible and the Koran, have been abrogated by the appearing of the new Manifestation, that is, their validity has been annulled. When God gives a new revelation, namely, the *Bayan* (which embraces the great mass of writings of the Bab), believers must refer to it alone for guidance. And as the divinely revealed books of previous dispensations are abrogated by the *Bayan,* so are the many books written by men who were followers of previous Manifestations. The Bab, therefore, forbade the reading of all non-Babi books, and commanded that they be burned. Believers must read only the *Bayan* and books written by eminent Babi scholars under the shadow of the *Bayan*. No one is permitted to own more than nineteen books, the first of which is to be the *Bayan,* the precepts of which will be binding on believers till the coming of Him-Whom-God-Will-Manifest. For the *Bayan* is the Straight Path of Truth. It is obligatory for the People of the *Bayan* to acquire knowledge and impart it to others. Every monarch to emerge in the Bayanic dispensation must choose twenty-five learned men to assist him in the furtherance of the Babi faith, and in going to the relief of the weak and needy.

Every family must entertain nineteen guests every nineteen days, even though they may be able to serve them nothing but water. The dead were to be washed once, or might be washed three to five times, and buried in stone coffins, with engraved rings on their fingers. After burial their graves must be visited by their friends once every nineteen-day month. The use of opium, alcohol, and tobacco was forbidden. Pack animals were not to be overloaded, and cows must not be used for riding, or for carrying loads. The milk of asses must not be drunk, and eggs must not be kept where they might spoil. The Bab also gave very complicated laws regarding inheritance. (See below, p. 62.)

Near the end of the *Arabic Bayan* the Bab wrote:

> The essence of religion in your beginning and return consists in your belief in God beside whom there is no god; then in Him-Whom-God-Will-Manifest on the Day of Resurrection in your return; then in the Book God will send down to him; then in Him-Whom-God-Has-Manifested under the name of . . . Sayyid Ali Muhammad the Bab; and then in that which God has sent down to him in the *Bayan*.

This, in brief, is the system of doctrine and of society and government which Sayyid Ali Muhammad believed God wished to establish through him in Iran and throughout the world. It seems that he realized the need for a spiritual and social reformation in his country, where at that time religion consisted largely of empty forms of worship, and where there was little knowledge of the true God, and little love for men. The reader may judge for himself the adequacy of the Bab's theology, and of his laws and precepts for establishing a just and effective social order for the world.

Whether the Bayanic system was given by revelation to the Bab from God, or whether it was the utopian dream of a man long in prison facing death, it never became a reality. No king ever adopted the Babi faith and used his authority to propagate it, and no nation ever attempted to order the life of its people in accordance with the laws of the *Bayan*. If the Bab was indeed, as he thought himself to be, a Major Manifestation of God, come to establish a new Theocratic Society which would take the place of Islam and all previous religious systems, and last for at least 1511 years, why were his high hopes for the future not realized? On the other hand, whatever one may think of his claims and his regulations, one cannot but admire the Bab for his devotion to the cause for which he gave his life.

4

The Vicegerency of Subh-i-Azal

IT IS THE BELIEF of the Shi'ite Muslims that shortly before
his death the Prophet Muhammad publicly appointed his
son-in-law Ali as his successor, or vicegerent, to become
the first Imam, and that Ali and each of the succeeding
Imams in like manner appointed the men who were to
succeed them as the leaders of the believers. Sayyid Ali
Muhammad, the Bab and the Point of the new Manifestation, realizing the certainty of his early death, followed the example of his ancestor Muhammad, the Point
of the preceding Manifestation, in naming his vicegerent.
Accordingly, after the execution of the Bab in Tabriz
on July 8, 1850, Mirza Yahya Subh-i-Azal became the
recognized head of the People of the *Bayan,* was accepted
by the Babi community as their divinely ordained ruler,
and continued in this position for some sixteen years.
Since the history of this period has unfortunately been
inaccurately related in some of the books purporting to
give a true account of the Babi and Baha'i movement,
it is necessary to present in some detail the established
facts.

Mirza Yahya, the successor of the Bab, was the son
of Mirza Buzurg of the district of Nur in the province
of Mazanderan. He was born in Teheran in 1831 A.D.
His father, according to the Babi historian, was "accom-
plished, wealthy, and much respected," but was not a

prince, as some have alleged. Mirza Yahya's mother and father died when he was a child, and he was committed to the care of his father's second wife, who, it is said, was warned in a dream of his future destiny, and showed him the greatest love and consideration. His education was supervised by his half-brother Mirza Husayn Ali, the son of Mirza Buzurg and his second wife, who was thirteen years older than Mirza Yahya. This half-brother later became known as Baha, and long after, in Akka, as Baha'u'llah. In his history of the Babi movement written about 1851, only a year after the execution of the Bab, Mirza Jani quotes the following statement which Mirza Husayn Ali had made regarding his younger brother:

> I busied myself with the instruction of Janab-i-Azal. The signs of his natural excellence and goodness of disposition were apparent in the mirror of his being. He ever loved gravity of demeanour, silence, courtesy, and modesty, avoiding the society of other children, and their behaviour. I did not, however, know that he would become the possessor of [so high] a station.

This statement shows how amicable the relations of the two brothers were shortly after the death of the Bab when Mirza Jani penned these words, and in what high esteem the elder held the younger.

When Mirza Yahya was still young, his brother used to bring followers of the Bab to his house in Teheran, and it was from their conversations that he first learned of the appearing of the "Lord of the Age." He read some of the Bab's writings, and became a believer about 1847. So great was his attachment to his Master, whom he had never seen, that when the Bab commanded his followers to go to Khurasan, the eastern province of Iran, the seventeen-year-old youth tried to obey, but was forbidden by his brother. Later, however, he went to Mazanderan, and on the way he met and became acquainted with Hazrat-i-Quddus, and accompanied him to Barfurush. There he met Qurratu'l-Ayn. Both leaders showed him great kindness and attention. Of this period Mirza Jani writes:

> I was in attendance on Janab-i-Azal in Mazanderan, night and day, for four months or more. . . . He was filled with ardour and ecstacy, and I found him ever disposed by nature to devotion and emancipation such that he utterly disregarded the world and its circumstances. . . . He showed a wonderful attachment to Hazrat-i-Quddus, and used often to read aloud with sweet utterance the homilies and prayers of that Master of the world.

When the news of the death of the Babi leader Hazrat-i-Quddus, fighting in the Mazanderan, reached Mirza Yahya, he fell ill for three days. Then, says Mirza Jani, "the signs of holiness appeared in his blessed form so that Janab-i-Azal became the blessed domain of the Will. . . ." Sometime after this Mirza Yahya sent a communication to the Bab in his prison in Chihriq. On reading it the Bab was overcome with joy, for, said he, "the *Bayan* has now borne fruit!" From this saying Mirza Yahya received the title, "His Highness the Fruit." At once the Bab appointed Mirza Yahya as his successor, giving him high titles. It seems that the title "Subh-i-Azal" (Morning of Eternity) by which the Bab's successor is best known, was given him because he rose to prominence in the fifth year of the Bab's Manifestation (1849) which, according to a well-known tradition, was characterized by the words, "A Light which shone from the Dawn of Eternity."

The Bab gave written notice of the appointment of Subh-i-Azal to the Letters of the Living who had survived the fighting in Mazanderan, and to other Babi leaders. He also sent some of his own personal effects, such as pencases, paper, writings, clothing, and rings to his successor-to-be, intending that "after him Subh-i-Azal should bear the divine influences." "He also wrote a testamentary deposition," says Mirza Jani, "explicitly nominating him [Azal] as his successor." On the death of the Bab, the Babi community accepted Subh-i-Azal and accorded him the high honor which the Bab had bestowed on him. There is not the slightest historical evidence dating from this period that anyone other than Subh-i-Azal was appointed or acted as successor to the Bab.

It was no easy task to which Subh-i-Azal, as yet only nineteen years of age, fell heir when his Master was executed. The Babis were still in arms against the Iranian government in Zanjan and in other parts of the country, and were feared and bitterly hated by the majority of the Muslim population. The Babis returned this hatred with interest, and considered both Nasiru'd-Din Shah and the mullas to be enemies of God and worthy of death because of their rejection of the Divine Manifestation. The new leader realized, however, that it was not expedient for the Babis to continue further this conflict with the government, and he issued orders for his followers to lay aside the sword. He was obeyed, and there were no more large uprisings after the ending of the Zanjan conflict. Subh-i-Azal made some journeys to visit scattered Babi communities to encourage the believers. He was busily occupied in arranging, transcribing, and circulating among believers the books of the Bab, and in teaching the Babi doctrines. Though the Prime Minister was very hostile to the Babis, it seems that for a time there was little open opposition to, or persecution of, the movement, which continued to grow after the execution of the Bab. It is impossible to estimate accurately the number of Babis in Iran at this time. There were perhaps some five thousand in Teheran. No doubt there were many times this number in the provinces. It was during this brief period of comparative quiet (1851-1852) that Mirza Jani wrote his history, *Nuqtatu'l-Kaf*, to which we have referred.

While temporarily free from attacks from without, the Babi community was disturbed by confusion within. Mirza Jani has described at length the curious phenomenon of the appearance of a number of men from among the Babis who revealed verses and claimed to be Manifestations of God, ignoring the Bab's statement that the next Manifestation would not come for at least 1511 years. Some of the Babis, jealous of the honor of their Master, Subh-i-Azal, wished to silence these claimants, but Mirza Jani states that Azal would not permit this, demanding only that they recognize his authority.

In spite of these internal problems, it seems that all went fairly well with the Babis till the summer of 1852, when an event which entirely altered the situation took place. For some time rumors had been going about the Teheran bazaar that the Shah was going to be killed. Finally, on August 15, as Nasiru'd-Din Shah was riding in the hills above Teheran on a hunting expedition, three men approached him as though they wished to present a petition. When they had come quite near, one of them drew a pistol and fired at the Shah, wounding him in the arm. Then they attempted to drag him from his horse and to cut his throat, but the Shah's retainers rushed up and saved him, killing one of the assassins and capturing the other two. When they were questioned the two captives confessed they were Babis, and said that their purpose was to avenge the death of the Bab. The man who was killed was the servant of Azim, a devoted disciple of the Bab who had been plotting against the government for some time. The Muslim historian says that Azim had induced twelve Babis to agree to take part in the assassination, but only three of them arrived on time. There is no doubt that this attempt on the life of the Shah was the result of a deliberate plot on the part of the Babis. The pistol had been charged with shot in

order that the assassins might fell the Shah, and then
kill him by cutting his throat, as they had been ordered
to do. The Shah, however, was not seriously wounded.

The excitement and confusion which followed may
be imagined. The gates of Teheran were guarded, and
a systematic search for the Babi leaders was made in
Teheran and throughout Iran; about thirty-five were
arrested. As the days went by the Shah became more and
more terrified over the situation in his kingdom, and
he resolved to make an exhibit of the Babis whom he
had gotten into his power. He accordingly divided them
up among the different classes of his subjects, giving
one to the Muslim clergy, another to the artillery, and
so on, informing all that the measure of their devotion
to their sovereign would be revealed by the zeal with
which they executed the offenders. It seems that several
of the prisoners were able to prove their innocence,
probably by denying that they were Babis, and were
released. It is possible that a number of those sentenced
to die had no direct part in the attempt on the life of
the Shah, but to be known as a Babi was sufficient to
be condemned.

On September 15, 1852, the executions were carried
out, each group trying to outdo the others in the bar-
barity with which they killed their unfortunate victims.
Twenty-eight Babis were killed, one of whom was the
beautiful and gifted Qurratu'l-Ayn, who had for some
time been under arrest and could not have been impli-
cated in the attempted assassination. Another was Mirza
Jani the historian. Most of the victims showed the greatest courage and devotion as they faced death, and their
bold testimony won many new converts to their Cause.
From this time on the Babis were more careful than
ever to conceal their faith, and were usually ready to
deny it when their lives were in danger. This practice
of dissimulation was approved by their leaders, as it
had been previously approved by the Shi'ites.

Subh-i-Azal and his brother Baha were not among
those who perished. The Shah attempted to arrest the
leader of the Babi movement, and offered a large re-
ward for his capture. But Subh-i-Azal managed to escape
in the garb of a dervish, and made his way to Baghdad
in Turkish territory, for he realized that he could no
longer live in his native land. After his flight two regi-
ments of royal troops raided his ancestral home in the
district of Nur in Mazanderan in order to capture him
and his followers; they arrested members of his family
and a number of his relatives and friends, bringing them
to Teheran, where many of them died in prison. Five
of the arrested persons, including Mirza Husayn Ali
(Baha), were kept in prison pending further investigation, there not being sufficient evidence to incriminate
them. After four months Baha was released. It has been
said that in order to save his life Baha denied that he
was a Babi, as the Bab had ordered his disciples to do at
the time of his execution. This is not improbable, for it
seems that those prisoners who were known to be Babis
were put to death, whether or not they were proved
guilty of implication in the plot to kill the Shah.

It appears that the Russian Legation in Teheran
helped to secure Baha's release on condition that he
leave Iran, and Baha later stated that both Russian and
Iranian officers accompanied him and his family when
he departed from Teheran one month after his release.
He arrived in Baghdad in April, 1853, where he joined
his brother Subh-i-Azal. Soon many other Babis followed
them to Baghdad.

From the beginning of 1853 till the spring of 1863
Baghdad was the seat of the Vicegerency of Subh-i-Azal,
and the center from which secret Babi propaganda was
carried on in Iran and Iraq. We do not possess a full
account of the happenings of these ten years, for there
was no historian like Mirza Jani to leave a reliable record
of events, but the main features of the story are clear.

The Babi community looked upon Subh-i-Azal as their supreme head, one in rank and authority with the Bab himself. Baha, however, was not satisfied with this situation. He probably realized that in order to survive the Babi Cause needed stronger leadership than his brother Azal was able to give, and he was confident that he could supply this need. But it was necessary for the leader to possess a divine appointment on which to base his authority. Did Baha have this? He had received no authority from the Bab, yet he had a growing conviction that he was the new Manifestation whose coming the Bab had predicted. It seems that he determined to make a claim for himself at some suitable time, and take over the leadership of the Cause. However, his attitude and conduct were displeasing to the other Babi leaders, who accused him of gathering about him a crowd of disreputable people to assist him in his purpose. Those who sided with Baha replied that the opposition of his brother and other Babis was the product of envy of Baha's increasing influence.

When, at the end of his first year in Baghdad, the Babi leaders severely rebuked Baha for his conduct, he became angry and left Baghdad in the night, telling no one, not even his own family, where he was going. For two years he lived as a dervish in the Kurdish mountains in northern Iraq. Finally, Subh-i-Azal discovered his whereabouts and wrote to him to return. Baha obeyed, wrote a letter of repentance to his brother, and came back to Baghdad in the spring of 1856.

Subh-i-Azal received and forgave his brother, and showed his confidence in him by delegating to Baha great authority, while he himself retired into greater seclusion. This arrangement, it seems, was in accordance with the command of the Bab, who shortly before his death had written a strong letter to Mirza Husayn Ali (Baha), charging him to take the best possible care of Subh-i-Azal lest any harm should come to him. And since the

Muslims of Baghdad were showing more and more hostility toward the Babis, Baha was able to convince his brother that it was not safe for him to appear in public or to see visitors. Also, this arrangement was agreeable to Subh-i-Azal's natural disposition.

Many of the Babi leaders were prolific writers, and Subh-i-Azal and his brother Baha were no exceptions; indeed, they exceeded them all. In later years Baha referred to the many "verses" he had composed in Baghdad, none of which is in existence. The only book of importance which he wrote while in Baghdad was the Persian *Iqan* (entitled *The Book of Certitude* in its English translation), which was composed around 1862. Its chief purpose was to prove that the Bab was a Major Manifestation of God, and the standpoint of the author is that of a loyal disciple. Little of the material in the book is original, for Baha merely repeats and elaborates the doctrines already taught by the Shaykhis and the Bab. He states that the interval between the Manifestations, including that between the Bab and the Manifestation to follow him, is "about 1000 years." However, from the insistence of his appeal in the *Iqan* to the Babis to accept Him-Whom-God-Will-Manifest, it seems that Baha was contemplating putting forth his own claim to superiority, though he had not yet done so.

In Baghdad Baha acquired some property, and he and Subh-i-Azal also acquired Ottoman nationality. With the abundant funds which came to Subh-i-Azal from the loyal Babis of Iran at his disposal, in accordance with the laws of the Bab, Baha was able to set up an impressive establishment with adequate facilities for extending hospitality to guests from Iran. His servants would go forth to meet the Shi'ite pilgrims who had come to Iraq to visit the shrines of the Imams, and would conduct them to Baha's center; there they would be entertained and instructed in the faith of the *Bayan*. The pilgrims would not usually even get a glimpse of the Vicegerent of the Bab, for access to Subh-i-Azal was obtained through his intermediary Baha, who often withheld permission under some pretext. Thus Subh-i-Azal, who lived in seclusion and rarely appeared in public, gradually decreased in importance in the eyes of the public as his aggressive older brother increased. To the Turkish officials, and no doubt to many of the Babis also, Baha now appeared to be the actual leader of the movement, although he still acted merely on behalf of Subh-i-Azal.

Baha was not the only one who was prepared to make a claim for himself at this time. A man named Mirza Asadullah of Khuy, surnamed Dayyan, who had been appointed by the Bab as amanuensis to Subh-i-Azal, declared that he was He-Whom-God-Will-Manifest, and some of the Babis became his followers. Baha held a long discussion with him, and Subh-i-Azal denounced him in a book he wrote, but as Dayyan remained obstinate he was murdered by Mirza Muhammad of Mazanderan, probably drowned in the Tigris River. Dayyan was not the only person thus eliminated by the Babis in Baghdad. There were several others who advanced similar claims, and the pretensions of these claimants naturally encouraged Baha to press his own claims, for to prevent chaos someone must be in control, and he had a better chance of success than anyone else. Hence, Baha continued to put himself forward. However, the opposition from the other Babi leaders was so fierce that he was forced to wait a while longer before openly declaring himself.

Meanwhile, the zealous Babis continued their efforts to convert the Shi'ite pilgrims on their way to visit the shrines of the Imams Ali and Husayn in Najaf and Karbala. This effort was bitterly resented by the Muslim religious leaders, and as a result there was fighting between the Muslims and the Babis. Finally, the Iranian government, incited by the Muslim mullas, intervened and requested the Turkish government to remove the

Babi leaders from Iraq. The Turkish government was quite ready to comply with this request, for the quarrels and fightings of the Babis and Muslims in Baghdad had no doubt caused great trouble for the authorities there. Accordingly, in May, 1863, Baha and his family left Baghdad for Istanbul, and were joined in Mosul by Subh-i-Azal who preceded them by two weeks. When they reached Istanbul, they were ordered to proceed yet farther west to the extreme border of Turkey, and to settle in the city of Edirne (Adrianople). They arrived there in December, 1863, and remained for four and one half years, far away from their native land.

5

The Schism Between Two Brothers

IN EDIRNE THE TASK which faced Subh-i-Azal, who for some sixteen years had been generally considered by the Babis to be the divinely appointed Head of the People of the *Bayan,* was by no means easy. The Babi community was disunified enough to require a firm hand to control it, and Subh-i-Azal totally lacked this. His older brother Baha had gradually come to occupy the place of actual leadership, though till now he had done everything in the name of Subh-i-Azal. However, about three years after reaching Edirne, probably in 1866, with no strong Babi leaders nearby to oppose him, Baha suddenly threw off the pretense of loyalty to his brother and made the claim which he had been contemplating for several years, that he was He-Whom-God-Will-Manifest, whose coming the Bab had predicted. He then called on Subh-i-Azal and all the Babis scattered over Turkey, Iran, Syria, and Egypt to acknowledge his supreme authority, and to accept as God's Word the revelations which he forthwith began to promulgate.

To understand the nature of Baha's claims, let us recall what the Bab wrote in the *Bayan* about Him-Whom-God-Will-Manifest, who would be another Major Manifestation. He would be divine, and his command would be God's command. He is not to be asked why he did anything. All previous Manifestations were for

him, and one verse of his writings would be better than
a thousand *Bayans*. He is to be recognized by himself.
Only God knows the time of his advent, but he will
not come prior to 1511 years, and not later than 2001
years, after the Bab. He will "reveal verses spontane-
ously and powerfully, without study and without the
means accessible to the learned. It is impossible that any
other than He . . . can lay claim to the command. . . ."
As we saw in the last chapter, a number of men made
claims for themselves but were rejected as pretenders
by the Babi leaders. Baha, however, because of his position of leadership under Subh-i-Azal and his relationship to Subh-i-Azal, had a better chance of success than
did the previous claimants. Accordingly, he advanced the
claim to be a Major Manifestation of Deity, the same
claim that the Bab had made some twenty-two years
earlier. Thus Baha not only seized the leadership of the
Babi community in Edirne but demanded that all recognize him as supreme ruler. It is said that he sent a letter
to Subh-i-Azal demanding his submission, but that his
brother refused. Thereupon Baha tried to force Subh-i-
Azal to yield by withholding his share of the allowances
which were paid by the Turkish government through
Baha for the Babis in Edirne. As a result, the family of
Subh-i-Azal lacked for food, and his little children became ill. His wife then went to complain to the wife of
the Turkish governor, an act deeply resented by Baha.

Though most of the People of the *Bayan* sooner or
later acknowledged Baha as He-Whom-God-Will-Manifest, Subh-i-Azal steadfastly refused to do so. He held
fast to the teachings of the Bab, believing that they were
the all-sufficient revelation of God for the present age,
and that they must be accepted and obeyed by multitudes of people for many centuries, before it would be
time for another Manifestation to appear. To Subh-i-
Azal, and the Babis who clung to him, it seemed utterly
unreasonable to believe that the elaborate system re-

vealed to the Bab by God could have been established for only twenty-two years. Had not the Bab indicated clearly in the *Bayan* that He-Whom-God-Will-Manifest would not come for at least 1511 years and might not come till 2001 years had passed? All the Babis were convinced that the Bab had been sent by God and was infallible. Since Subh-i-Azal had been appointed as the successor by the Bab himself, was not he also sent by God, as they had for sixteen years believed? And did he not possess divine wisdom, and was he not one with the Bab? How then could it be possible that Subh-i-Azal should be unable to recognize Him-Whom-God-Will-Manifest when he appears? But Subh-i-Azal rejected the claim of his brother to be "He." Hence, for those Babis who accepted Baha, and later became known as Baha'is, there was no alternative except to say that the Bab, who was divinely inspired and knew all things, had deliberately chosen as his vicegerent a man who was to become the "Point of Darkness," the chief enemy of Him-Whom-God-Will-Manifest.

In their effort to escape this dilemma, Baha and his partisans did two things: first, they got rid of most of the leading Babis who sided with Subh-i-Azal; and second, they rewrote many of the Babi writings and records, and also the history of the Babi movement, largely ignoring Subh-i-Azal, greatly magnifying the position of Baha as a Major Manifestation and degrading the Bab to the role of "forerunner" for Baha, who was the real Manifestation for the age.

Though this sad chapter of the history has been largely omitted by the Baha'i historians, the truth is that about twenty of the Babis who remained faithful to Subh-i-Azal, later known as Azalis or Babis, were murdered in Baghdad, Edirne, and Akka by the followers of Baha. Two of the slain were brothers of Fatima the widow of the Bab, and one was her husband Sayyid Muhammad of Isfahan. Two more were Letters appoint-

ed by the Bab. It has been said that these assassinations
were the work of the too-zealous followers of Baha, and
that he was not himself responsible. However this may
be, one might expect that a person who possessed the
divine knowledge and power to influence men which
Baha claimed to have, would have been able to prevent
such acts by his intimate disciples. And could he not
have disowned them, or at least punished them, for their
deeds? As far as is known he did neither.

According to the Azalis, Baha not only sanctioned the
murder of the Babis who refused to accept him, but also
attempted to have his brother Subh-i-Azal poisoned.
The Baha'is replied that it was Subh-i-Azal who tried to
poison Baha. A careful study of the evidence indicates
that the charges against Subh-i-Azal cannot be substan-
tiated. Whatever the truth of the matter, both sides
agree that an attempt was made by one of the brothers
to poison the other.

Finally, the conflict between the two unequal parties
became so fierce that the Turkish authorities decided to
separate them, and apparently without making any effort
to determine who was in the right, they sent all the Babi
exiles away from Edirne in August, 1868. Subh-i-Azal,
his family, and a few followers were sent to Cyprus, and
Baha and his family and followers were sent to Akka
(Acre) in Palestine, both regions being at that time
under Turkish rule. In order to keep informed concerning the activities of the exiles, the authorities detailed
four Baha'is to go to Cyprus to spy on Subh-i-Azal, and
four Azalis to spy on Baha in Akka. One of the Azalis was
murdered by the Baha'is before leaving Edirne, and the
other three were murdered soon after their arrival in
Akka.

Since the great majority of the Babis became followers of Baha, our principal concern from now on will be
with the Baha'i branch of the Babi movement which had
Akka for its center and Baha for its head. However,

before leaving Subh-i-Azal and his small minority of disciples, we will relate briefly the story of his later life. With his two wives and his children and a few followers he reached Famagusta on the island of Cyprus. All were under sentence of life imprisonment, and were given a daily allowance by the Turkish government. In 1878 Cyprus passed from Turkish to British control, and the Azali prisoners became pensioners of the British government. Living thus in isolation, Subh-i-Azal was almost completely forgotten.

Subh-i-Azal lived to the age of eighty-one, and died in Famagusta on April 29, 1912. An account of his death and burial has been published, written by one of his sons, who on becoming a Christian renamed himself "Constantine the Persian." Subh-i-Azal left no Will, and appointed no successor; his followers have carried on no propaganda. However, there are in Iran several thousand people who consider themselves Babis, and who believe that in this schism the right was with Subh-i-Azal.

6

The Manifestation of Baha'u'llah

BAHA, NOW RESIDING as a political prisoner in Akka with about seventy of his family and adherents who had been deported with him from Edirne, began to play his new role as a Divine Manifestation and ruler of the great majority of the Babis scattered throughout the Near East. The problem which he had to solve was not merely one of succession to the leadership of the Babi movement, but whether the religion which he represented was to become a world religion addressed to all mankind, or was to remain only an obscure Persian sect. For while the Bab had confidently predicted the time when his religion would cover the earth, it had already become clear to Baha that the system outlined by the Bab could never make any headway outside Iran. Many of the laws laid down by the Bab were entirely unsuited to the needs of mankind, either in Iran or out of it, and the hope of forcibly establishing a Babi theocracy had proved impossible to fulfil. Accordingly, Baha, while not abrogating the *Bayan* of the Bab, adopted a policy of ignoring some of the impractical aspects of the Babi system and its connection with Shi'ite Islam, and of emphasizing the universal character of the religion of which he had become the head. As he moved westward, he came to lands in which many Christians and Jews resided. Hence he undertook to attract them to himself, as well as Babis and Muslims. One way in which he did this was by issuing numerous epistles, or Tablets, as they were called, in which he set forth his claim to be a Manifestation of God, and commanded people to accept and obey him.

In Akka Baha had ample leisure to meditate, and to prepare the proofs for his claim to be a new Manifestation. The Bab had adduced his "verses" as the proof that he spoke for God, and in like manner Baha issued Tablets and other pronouncements which he said were the Words of God. But these supposedly inspired utterances did not convince everyone that their author was truly the He-Whom-God-Will-Manifest predicted by the Bab, and so Baha used all his erudition and ingenuity to produce other bases for his claims to Divinity. He searched for an adequate title befitting his claims. Long before he had been given the title "Baha" (Splendor, or Glory). Now he chose a phrase found in the *Bayan,* namely, "Baha'u'llah (The Glory of God), and he is known by this name today. According to the *Bayan,* this is a title for each of the Divine Manifestations. In the *Bayan* the Bab pronounced it "the best of names," assuming it for himself, and bestowing it on Subh-i-Azal. Claiming all occurrences of the title "Baha" in sacred books as references to himself, Mirza Husayn Ali frequently read the passages out of context, and usually failed to state the chapter and verse from which he was quoting. Thus he often appropriated to himself inapplicable words and statements.

The Azalis who had been sent to spy on the Baha'is began after a time to cause them great annoyance by attempting to arouse the natives of Akka against them. The Muslims of Akka were all Sunnites, and were quite intolerant of heretics such as the Baha'is. Therefore, in order to avoid trouble, Baha'u'llah and his followers took great pains to conceal their real beliefs and to publicly profess and practice the faith of Islam. Accordingly, they went regularly to the Muslim mosques and recited the prayers after the manner of the Sunnites. They also kept the Muslim month of fasting, Ramazan, and tried in every way possible to convince the Muslims that they were one with them. So successful were they in this effort that when Baha'u'llah and his son and successor Abbas Effendi died, the Sunnite clergy conducted their funeral services. This they would never have done had they realized that Baha'u'llah claimed to be a Manifestation of God greater than Muhammad. The title "Baha'u'llah," the Splendor of God, was therefore carefully avoided in Akka, and the leader of the Baha'is was known as Baha Effendi, or Baha'u'Din, the Splendor of Religion. But this attempt to conceal the nature of their faith was being thwarted by the Azalis, who began to circulate some of the verses of Baha'u'llah, with interpolations of their own, among the people of Akka.

Finally, the Baha'is determined to get rid of the trouble-makers. On January 23, 1872, seven of the Baha'is came upon three of the Azalis in a house in Akka and murdered them. Though some Baha'i writers have entirely omitted this part of their history, there is no doubt whatever that the assassinations took place. Whether this deed was done at the command of Baha'u'llah, or was contrary to his orders, is uncertain.

The Turkish authorities at once arrested Baha'u'llah and his sons and most of the male members of the Baha'i community, and confined them for several days. Baha'u'llah and his sons were soon released. The seven murderers were sent to the harbor, where they were kept in prison for some years, and later freed. Sixteen other Baha'is were kept in prison for six months, and then released.

While Subh-i-Azal and Baha'u'llah were enduring life imprisonment in distant lands, most of the Babis in Iran had become Baha'is, and were sometimes persecuted by the Muslims. Others had become Azalis, and were opposed by both Muslims and Baha'is. Ever since the massacre which followed the Babi attempt on the life of the Shah in 1852, Babis had practiced "concealment" in order to live their lives in peace among their unbelieving neighbors. Little is known about the numbers or activities of these people who, when recognized, were generally despised as heretics. During these years there were occasional outbursts of opposition, with a few murders. Some Muslims who wished to get rid of their personal enemies would do so by branding them as "Babis," and getting them killed. A Baha'i writer has stated that about thirty-one Baha'is were killed in Iran and Iraq between the years 1866 and 1891. It is not known how many Azalis were killed by Baha'is and Muslims, but the number was not large. The statements often heard about the many thousands of Baha'i martyrs in Iran are entirely false.

Muslim historians relate that Muhammad sent letters from Medina to the kings of Persia, Byzantium, and other countries, bidding them to acknowledge him as a Prophet of Allah. Following this example Baha'u'llah, probably during the early part of his residence in Akka, composed a number of epistles which he addressed to numerous rulers. To the Czar of Russia he said, "One of thy ambassadors did assist me when I was in prison, in chains and fetters [in Teheran in 1852]. Therefore hath God decreed unto thee a station which the knowledge of no one comprehendeth." He praised Queen Victoria for abolishing slavery and establishing representative government. He violently denounced the Sultan of Turkey for the wrongs done to him and his followers in Akka. In the Epistle to the Shah of Iran the Shah is severely rebuked for killing the Bab, and the Babi attempt to assassinate him is excused if not approved. To the Pope, Baha'u'llah proclaims himself as God the Father, as the Comforter promised by Christ, and as Christ himself come again, and bids the Pope and all Christians to accept him. "Dost thou dwell in palaces," he asks the Pope, "while the King of Manifestations is in the most ruined of abodes [Akka]? Leave palaces to those who desire them, then advance to the Kingdom with spirituality and fragrance." At this or a later time Baha'u'llah also addressed messages to America, Austria, and Germany. There is no evidence that any of these epistles was ever sent, or received by those to whom they were addressed. It is inconceivable that a subject of Turkey, banished to Akka as a political prisoner, should send a letter like the one Baha'u'llah wrote to his Sultan. It is evident that the purpose of these eloquent epistles, known as the *Alwah-i-Salatin* (Epistles of the Kings) was to impress the Baha'is with the boldness of their Master. This purpose was fully achieved.

After a severe imprisonment of several months in the military barracks and an eight-year residence in various rented houses in the town of Akka, Baha'u'llah rented a palace several miles outside of Akka in 1877. In 1880 he first rented, and later bought, the Bahji Palace, in which he lived with his family and three of his sons, while his eldest son Abbas Effendi, with his family and sister, remained at Akka. "Sometimes he used to visit the town, and while he dwelt outside the town, visitors, whether pilgrims or Companions, had the honour of seeing him after permission had been obtained, and used to spend some days and nights there." While Baha'u'llah was not free to leave the district, he was given a great deal of freedom to move about Akka and its environs as he pleased. He was by no means "in prison" during most of his sojourn there. The palaces and beautiful gardens which Baha'u'llah bought were made possible by the large sums of money and generous gifts which came to him from his faithful followers in Iran and other lands.

During his years in Akka, contrary to his custom when he was in Baghdad and Edirne, Baha'u'llah lived largely in seclusion. No one was allowed to visit him except by special permission. Each visitor was carefully prepared for his audience with the Manifestation of God. He was told that what he saw when he came into the Divine Presence would depend on what he was himself — if he was a material person he would see only a man, but if he was a spiritual being he would see God. When his expectations had been sufficiently aroused, the pilgrim was led into the presence of Baha'u'llah and was permitted to gaze for a few moments upon "the Blessed Perfection," care being taken that the visitation should end before the spell was broken.

The location of Baha'u'llah in Akka, which was nearer to Iran than Edirne, no doubt helped to accelerate the growth of Baha'ism. From the time he was taken to Akka, many of his followers began making the pilgrimage there in the hope of seeing their Lord. Baha'u'llah, however, did not encourage the Baha'is in their desire to visit him. First of all, there was too great a risk of their seeing and hearing things in Akka which might weaken their faith. There was a saying among the Baha'is of Iran that whoever went to Akka lost his faith. Also, the presence of large numbers of zealous believers in the city would undoubtedly have led to complications with the native Muslim population. The Baha'is in other lands were therefore told that if they gave to Baha'u'llah the money they would have spent on their journey, they would gain the same merit as if they had come before his Presence.

However, the intimate relationship between Baha'u'llah and his followers was carefully maintained. Personal epistles, or Tablets, which were sent to the believers in Iran and other lands, answering their questions and praising them for their fidelity to the Cause, took the place of personal visits. These letters were all carried by hand, as it was dangerous to entrust them to the posts. The Baha'i who received an epistle from his Master was indeed a fortunate man. He would show it to his brothers in the faith, who would kiss it and ask for copies, and

he would then lay it away among his choicest treasures.
The secluded life which Baha'u'llah led gave him ample
opportunity to dictate these epistles. He composed a vast
number of them, in addition to numerous longer treatises. The Baha'is believed all of these writings to be
the Word of God.

Baha'u'llah lived in Akka or its suburbs for twenty-
four years. During this period the numbers and influence
of the Baha'is in Iran and in other lands continued to
increase. One estimate placed their number in Iran in
1892 as five hundred thousand, but since there was no
census, and since the Baha'is concealed their faith, no
accurate figures were possible. Usually Bahai's were able
to live in peace with their Muslim neighbors, and as long
as they did not stir up trouble they were rarely molested.
To the present day, the Iranian government has recognized four religions, Zoroastrianism, Judaism, Christianity, and Islam, but not Baha'ism; Baha'is in Iran have
been officially classed as Muslims.

During the final period of Baha'u'llah's life, his followers noted that he was often overcome by sadness.
This was not due to any financial difficulties, for Baha'-
u'llah had been able to provide well for himself and his
family with funds which his agents collected for him.
He purchased lands for each of his four sons in villages
in the vicinity of Akka, as well as in the Galilee and
Haifa districts, and had these properties registered in
their names. But there were other problems in his family
which gave him concern. He foresaw the trouble which
Munira Khanum, the wife of Abbas Effendi, might
cause, and he charged his three younger sons to guard
his writings carefully lest any of them fall into her hands
and be destroyed by her. He no doubt also realized that
there would be another power struggle after his death,
similar to the one which had caused his banishment to
Akka.

At length Baha'u'llah fell ill, and died on May 29, 1892, at the age of seventy-four. His body was buried according to the rites of the Sunnite Muslims in the house of his son-in-law Sayyid Ali Afnan in the Bahji Garden, and his tomb soon became a shrine for the Baha'is who visit Akka.

7

The Doctrines and Decrees
of Baha'u'llah

IT IS IMPOSSIBLE in one chapter to give more than an outline of the teachings of Baha'u'llah. Like the Bab and Subh-i-Azal, he was a prolific writer, and during a period of some thirty years he is said to have composed more than one hundred volumes and countless epistles. Most of his writings were addressed to individuals or groups of believers who had asked him questions, and were usually not very lengthy. These were called Tablets. Some were written in Persian, some in Arabic, often in a style which is difficult to understand. No collection of all these writings has been made, or could be made. However, all are considered by Baha'is to be the Word of God. The Baha'is have no definite canon of Scripture, as do Jews, Christians, and Muslims. Some of the writings of Baha'u'llah have been translated into other languages, and are being circulated outside the Arabic and Persian areas, so it is now possible for a larger number of readers to become acquainted with his doctrines and commandments and exhortations. Notably, a large and well-edited book entitled *Bahai Scriptures,* more than half of which consists of writings of Baha'u'llah, was published in 1923 with the approval of the Baha'i Committee on Publications in America. More recently, another compilation of his writings and those of his son Abdu'l-Baha has been published by the Baha'i Publishing Trust under the title *Baha'i World Faith*. This book "has been compiled," according to the editor, "to replace the work published in 1923 . . . and contains later and more accurate translations." The reader is referred to these volumes for first-hand acquaintance with Baha'u'llah's teachings.

The theological background of the Baha'i faith is the same as that of the *Bayan* of the Bab. Like the Bab, Baha'u'llah taught that God is unknowable except through his Manifestations. Baha'u'llah considered the Great Manifestations to be those referred to by the Bab, namely, Adam, Noah, Abraham, Moses, Jesus, and Muhammad. Having himself been a Babi, and knowing that he and all the other early Babis had considered the Bab to be a Major Manifestation of God who had taken the place of Muhammad, Baha'u'llah did not deny this belief. However, he sought to lessen the status of the Bab by frequently referring to him as "my forerunner," and he made it appear that the chief function of the Bab was to prepare the way for him, a much greater Manifestation. Baha'u'llah claimed to be He-Whom-God-Will-Manifest, and took for himself all the high titles and divine attributes which the Bab in the *Bayan* had said the coming Manifestation would possess. He also said he was the "return" of the Imam Husayn of the Shi'ites. Also he claimed to be the "return" of Jesus Christ, and the Comforter promised by Christ, as well as the Manifestation of God the Father. Though the Bab undertook to establish a universal religion, he directed his appeal almost entirely to the Shi'ite Muslims. Baha'u'llah, however, extended his invitation to Jews, Christians, and Zoroastrians as well, and appealed to them from their own Scriptures. The position which Baha'u'llah claimed for himself was not merely that of teacher or prophet, but that of God. Hence, his words purported to be not those of man, but of God himself.

Baha'u'llah claimed to have knowledge which no one

else possesses, or is able to possess. He said that nothing can move between heaven and earth without his permission. He claimed to be infallible in everything. To quote from the *Bahai Scriptures*:

> If He declares water to be wine, or heaven to be earth, or light to be fire, it is true and there is no doubt therein; and no one has the right to oppose Him, or to say "why" or "wherefore". . . . Verily no account shall be demanded of Him for what He shall do. . . . Verily if He declares the right to be left, or the south to be north, it is true and there is no doubt therein. Verily He is to be praised in His deeds and to be obeyed in His command. He hath no associate in His behest and no helper in His power; He doeth whatsoever He willeth, and commandeth whatever He desireth.

Since Baha'u'llah had claimed to be He-Whom-God-Will-Manifest, it was to be expected that he would at once abrogate the *Bayan,* and give his followers a new Book from God. Strange as it may seem, there is no evidence whatever that Baha'u'llah attempted to do this. On the contrary, in Baghdad in 1862, Baha'u'llah wrote a letter in which he said: "I swear by God that if any of the people of the *Bayan* [Babis] was to mention that the Book [*Bayan*] is abrogated, may God break the mouth of the speaker and the calumniator."

Then, if the *Bayan* is not abrogated, are its laws binding on Baha'is as well as on Babis? Such questions continued to come to Baha'u'llah after he reached Akka, and he accordingly supplied the answer. As he wrote near the end of his life:

> His Holiness the Forerunner [the Bab] revealed laws. But the word of command was dependent on acceptance. Therefore, this wronged one [Baha'u'-llah] implemented some of them, and revealed them in *Al-Kitab Al-Aqdas* couched in other terms. . . . Some laws of new doctrines were also revealed.

This book, which he named the Most Holy Book, perhaps because in both Arabic and Persian the Bible is called the Holy Book, was composed in 1872, or soon after. It was written in the Arabic language, like the Koran, though most of the Baha'is at that time were Iranians to whom Arabic was a foreign language. The *Aqdas,* as the book is frequently called, is small, about the size of the Gospel of Mark, but it is the most important of all the Baha'i literature. Of all his books Baha'u'llah referred to it alone in his Will. Likewise, his son Abbas Effendi (Abdu'l-Baha) wrote in his Last Will and Testament: "Unto the Most Holy Book everyone must turn, and all that is not expressly recorded therein must be referred to the Universal House of Justice." And Shoghi Effendi, the great-grandson of Baha'u'llah, the first Guardian of the Cause, states that this little volume "may rank as the most signal act of His [Baha'u'llah's] ministry." "This *Most Holy Book,*" he continues,

> whose provisions must remain inviolate for no less than a thousand years, and whose system will embrace the entire planet, may well be regarded as the brightest emanation of the mind of Baha'u'llah, as the Mother Book of His Dispensation, and the Charter of His New World Order.

The Most Holy Book was not printed for a number of years after it was written, since it was no doubt impossible to publish such a book in Syria where Baha'u'llah could not openly make known his claims. After some years the author authorized his son Mirza Muhammad Ali and Mirza Aqa Jan of Kashan (called the "Servant of God") to revise the *Aqdas* and other sacred writings, and to take them to Bombay and supervise their publication. This was done in 1890. The *Iqan* and other books as well as the *Kitab-i-Aqdas* were also published for the first time. Since all these writings were revised prior to publication, their present form must be dated near the end of the Akka period of the life of Baha'u'llah, and, while he no doubt approved textual changes made by the revisers, the works cannot be considered the work of Baha'u'llah alone.

In view of what the founder and leaders of the Baha'i movement have said about the unique importance of the *Aqdas*, it is surprising, to say the least, that no authorized translation of the whole *Aqdas* by Baha'i scholars has yet been published, either in Persian, the language of Iran, or in any other language. In *Bahai Scriptures*, there are found among the 262 pages filled with the words of Baha'u'llah only a few brief paragraphs taken from the Most Holy Book. Likewise in the later publication *Baha'i World Faith*, the *Aqdas* is referred to only six times in the index, and the book contains no quotations of any length from this "brightest emanation of the mind of Baha'u'llah." It is almost impossible to obtain an Arabic copy of the *Aqdas*, and the headquarters of the Baha'i Faith in America has stated in writing that it has never had a copy of the book. In 1944 Shoghi Effendi, the Guardian of the Cause, stated that "the codification of the *Kitab-i-Aqdas*, the Mother-Book of the Baha'i Revelation, and the systematic promulgation of its laws and ordinances, are as yet unbegun." But more important than a codification is an authorized translation, and a scholarly Baha'i translation of this book is long overdue.

Realizing the importance of the *Kitab-i-Aqdas* in the Baha'i system, several western scholars have published translations of portions of the book. However, no complete translation into English had been made till 1961, when Dr. E. E. Elder, a competent Arabic scholar, assisted by several scholars with an intimate knowledge of Baha'i terminology and beliefs, published *al-Kitab al-Aqdas*, an accurate and readable translation of the whole book, with introduction and notes. The text is included in full in a seventy-two-page appendix to *The*

Baha'i Faith, by William M. Miller.* In the volume in hand, space permits only a brief summary of the more important topics treated, with a few quotations to acquaint the reader with the author's style and imagery.

The book begins with a statement regarding the necessity of knowing Baha'u'llah. "Whoever attains unto Him attains unto all good, and whoever is deprived of Him is of the people of error, even though he perform all [good] works."

The author then enjoins obedience to the commands which follow, saying:

> From My stipulations there passes the sweet smell of my gown, and by them the standards of victory are erected on hillocks and hills. The tongue of My power has spoken in the might of My greatness, addressing My people, [saying], "Perform My stipulations out of love for My beauty "

First there come regulations for worship. "Worship has been ordained for you — nine prostrations to God, who sent down the verses. Whenever you desire to worship, turn your face toward My most holy direction." Babi worship consists of nineteen prostrations at noon facing Shiraz. The worship ordained by Baha'u'llah is briefer, and is to be performed three times each day, between sunrise and noon, between noon and late afternoon, and between sunset and two hours after sunset. The words to be repeated are not given in the *Aqdas*. The worshipper is to face the place where Baha'u'llah resides, which is Akka.

As in the *Bayan*, all congregational worship is abolished, except in the case of prayers for the dead. All men and women above the age of fifteen must say the prayers, but the old and sick are excused. Travellers

*Published by William Carey Library (see Preface).

are to make one prostration only, or if this is impossible, to say, "Praise be to God!" After completing the required prostrations, the worshipper is to sit on the floor with feet crossed under him and hands on his knees, and repeat eighteen times, "Praise be to God, the Possessor of the kingdoms of this world and the next!" All the prayers are to be said in Arabic.

Then follow the regulations for fasting. "O multitude of creation, we have ordained the Fast for you, certain limited days. After the completion of them we have made al-Nayruz [No Ruz] a feast for you." In his arrangements for the Fast Baha'u'llah adopted what the Bab had prescribed in the *Bayan,* as follows: The year is to be divided into nineteen months of nineteen days each (19 x 19 = 361). The nineteenth month is the month of the Fast. Immediately following the Fast comes the ancient Iranian festival of No Ruz (New Year), which is to be observed with joy and gladness. The four or five intercalary days are placed between the eighteenth and nineteenth months, and are to be spent entertaining relations and friends, and feeding the poor. During the nineteen days of the Fast, no food or drink is to be taken from sunrise till sunset. The Baha'i Fast is, therefore, less severe than that of Islam, which lasts for twenty-eight days.

Each day every believer should wash his hands, then his face, and having seated himself facing God (toward Akka) should repeat ninety-five times, *"Allahu Abha!"* (God is Most Splendid). "In like manner, perform ablutions before Worship because of a command from God." Murder, adultery, back-biting, and calumniation are unlawful.

Then follows the law of Inheritance as given by the Bab. According to the *Bayan,* the property of the deceased must be divided into nine unequal parts. Two parts are to be used for funeral expenses, and the balance is then to be divided into forty-two equal parts of which (1) children will receive nine, (2) husbands or wives eight, (3) fathers seven, (4) mothers six, (5) brothers five, (6) sisters four, and (7) teachers three. This division, however, was changed by Baha'u'llah. He says that when he heard the protests of unborn children saying that they would not get enough of the inheritance, he doubled their share, and reduced the shares of others. How this was to be done is not stated in the *Aqdas*. When there are no heirs to the portions for any of the above classes, their shares are to go to the House of Justice. It would be interesting to know how many loyal Baha'is have been able to divide their possessions in accordance with this scale during the century since this law was given.

Next, provision is made for the House of Justice. In every city there shall be a House of Justice, "and the souls according to *al-Baha* will assemble in it." The numerical value of the Arabic letters in *Baha'* is nine, hence the House of Justice must have nine or more members. They are to be God's stewards, and must consult about the welfare of men for the sake of God.

Then comes a warning against any one who may falsely claim to be a Manifestation:

> Whoever claims Command before the completion of a thousand years is a false liar. . . . Whoever explains this verse or interprets it in any other way than that plainly sent down, he will be deprived of the Spirit and Mercy of God. . . . Fear God and follow not your illusions.

In this statement Baha'u'llah made it clear that his dispensation would last till at least A.D. 2866.

Next, believers are told not to be troubled "when the sun of My beauty goes down and the heaven of My temple is hidden," that is, when Baha'u'llah dies; they must rise up and help the Cause. They are warned against pride of wealth and position.

It is incumbent on every father to provide proper education for his sons and daughters. If he fails to do so, the House of Justice must supervise their education, using charity funds for this purpose when necessary. "Whoever educates his son or anyone's sons, it is as though he had educated one of My sons."

While Baha'u'llah lives, disputed points are to be referred to him for settlement. After his death they are to be referred to his writings. "O people," he says, "do not be troubled when the kingdom of My Manifestation has disappeared. . . . In My Manifestation there is wisdom, and in My Disappearance there is another wisdom." Then comes the punishment for the murderer and the incendiary. "Whoever burns a house intentionally, burn him. Whoever kills a person with intent, kill him."

The regulations for marriage fill several pages of the *Aqdas.* "God has ordained marriage for you. Beware lest you go beyond two [wives], and whoever is satisfied with one of the handmaidens, his soul is at rest and so is hers." All must marry, that there may be born "those who will make mention of Me among My creatures." People are warned not to corrupt the earth with immorality. If trouble arise between husband and wife, he must not divorce her within a year. If after a year the wound is not healed "there is no harm in divorce." As in Islam, no provision is made for a woman to divorce her husband.

Traffic in slaves is forbidden. Believers must adorn themselves "with the beautiful garments of [good] works." "Let no one oppose another; nor one person kill another. . . . Do you kill him whom God brought to life through a Spirit from Him?"

Baha'u'llah then addresses various kings and rulers of the earth, and exhorts them to accept him. "By God," he says, "we do not desire to take possession of your kingdoms, but we have come to possess your hearts. . . . Blessed is the king who arises to help My cause in My kingdom and cuts himself off from all but me!" The king of Austria (the Emperor Franz Joseph) is rebuked because he passed Akka on his way to Jerusalem (in 1869) without stopping to inquire about Baha'u'llah. To the king of Berlin (probably Wilhelm I) he says, "Beware lest conceit keep thee from the Rising-place of Manifestation and passion screen thee from the Possessor of the Throne and the Earth." To the rulers of America he says,

> O kings of America and chiefs of the multitude in it, hear what the Dove on the branches of Continuing Eternity warbles, saying, "There is no god besides Me, the Continuing, the Forgiving, the Generous." Adorn the temple [body] of the Kingdom with the garment of Justice and Piety, and its head with the crown of the Remembrance of your Lord.

The Ottoman Empire is severely rebuked and threatened, no doubt because of its treatment of the writer.

The address to Iran is most conciliatory, though it was there that the Babis had suffered most:

> O land of al-Ta [Teheran], do not be sorrowful for anything. God has made thee the Rising-place of the Joy of the worlds. If He Wills, He will bless thy throne through him who rules with justice and gathers the sheep of God which have been scattered by wolves. . . . Rejoice thou in that God has made thee the Horizon of Light since the Rising-place of Manifestation [Baha'u'llah] was born in thee and thou art called by this Name.

Since the *Aqdas* was not published till 1890 A.D., and was not translated from Arabic, it is improbable that any of the kings and rulers addressed therein ever read or heard of the messages intended for them.

There are to be two great festivals. The first commemorates the declaration of Baha'u'llah. The date for this is not given in the *Aqdas*, but it is observed by

Baha'is in the Feast of Rizwan from April 21 to May 2. The second festival "is the day on which We sent Him who should tell the people the Good News of this Name by which the dead are raised," that is, the declaration of the Bab, which was on May 23. It is noteworthy that Baha'u'llah here refers to the Bab, not as a previous Manifestation, but as one whom he had sent to tell the good news of his coming.

In addition to the above, the *Aqdas* contains injunctions concerning cleanliness, the importance of work, religious endowments and taxes, punishments for various crimes, hospitality, the burial of the dead, and many other things.

Near the conclusion Baha'u'llah gives an important command: "O people of Creation, whenever the dove flies from the forest of praise and makes for the furthermost hidden goal, then refer what you did not understand in the Book to the Bough which branches from the Self-Subsistent Stock." That is, after the death of Baha'u'llah, questions about the interpretation of his Book are to be referred to his son, but he does not state which son.

The Most Holy Book ends with these words: "Fear God, O people of intelligence, By My Most Great, Most Holy, High, and Most Splendid Name!"

As one studies the *Aqdas* it becomes clear that, while it contains numerous ethical and religious teachings which might be followed in any society anywhere, it also contains numerous laws which presuppose the existence of a Baha'i State, with an executive, a judiciary, and a police force. How else could taxes and fines be collected, and crimes be punished by imprisonment and death? Baha'u'llah definitely anticipated the time when the "People of Baha" like the People of Islam would establish a regime in which Religion and State became one. The Most Holy Book is supposed to contain the basic laws for this world Theocratic-State for the coming one thousand or more years.

A careful comparison of the laws of the *Aqdas* with those given by the Bab in the *Bayan* will show that many of Baha'u'llah's provisions are identical with, or modifications of, provisions previously given by the Bab. As one scholar has said, "The *Aqdas* is a rehash of the *Bayan*."

Though strangely unmentioned in the *Aqdas,* one of the most widely publicized principles of Baha'u'llah is that of World Peace. In his early *Epistle to Kings* (c. 1867) Baha'u'llah wrote: "Be at peace with one another, and reduce your armies that your expenses may be diminished." This is perhaps the first of his many appeals for World Peace. War was a present and disturbing reality for Baha'u'llah. The Crimean War was fought while he was in Baghdad; in 1870 France was defeated by Prussia, and in 1877 Turkey was defeated by Russia. Peace Congresses had been held a number of times in Europe, and Baha'u'llah was doubtless aware of and in sympathy with these efforts. He foretold the time when "these fruitless strifes and ruinous wars would pass away, and the Most Great Peace would come." This prediction, sad to say, has not yet been fulfilled.

Some of the finest of Baha'u'llah's words found in his various writings are the following:

> All of you are the fruit of one Tree and the leaves of one Branch. It is not for him who loves his country to be proud, but [rather] for him who loves the whole world.
>
> By the Most Great Name, if one of the Companions vexeth any one, it is as though he had vexed God Himself. Ye are forbidden strife, quarreling, sedition, murder and the like thereof with a stringent prohibition in God's Book.
>
> O people of God, do not concern yourselves with yourselves: take thought for the reformation of the world and the purification of its peoples. The refor-

mation of the world will be [effected] by good and
pure deeds and gracious and well-pleasing virtues.

What has attracted many persons in various lands to
Baha'u'llah has not been that he rendered some unique
service to humanity, and not the laws which he promul-
gated for his proposed Baha'i Theocracy, but rather these
ethical and humanitarian teachings regarding peace and
unity among the people of the world.

8

The Rule of Abdu'l-Baha

JUST AS THE BAB, following the Shi'ite principle by which each Prophet and Imam appointed his successor, designated Subh-i-Azal to succeed him, so Baha'u'llah in like manner named his successor. Some years before his death he indicated in the *Kitab-i-Aqdas* that he was to be succeeded by "him whom God has meant, who has branched from this ancient Root." By this he meant that his successor was to be his son, but he did not specify which of his four sons was intended. However, before his death Baha'u'llah clarified this important matter in his Will and Testament, in which he said: "The reference in this blessed verse is to the Most Mighty Branch ["Ghusn-i-A'zam," the title for Abbas Effendi]." Then he continued: "Verily, God hath decreed the station of the Most Great Branch ["Ghusn-i-Akbar," the title for Mirza Muhammad Ali] after the station of the former. Verily, He is the Commanding One, the Wise."

From this passage it is clear that it was Baha'u'llah's intention that he should be succeeded by his eldest son Abbas Effendi, a man about fifty years old at the death of his father, and that Abbas Effendi should be succeeded by another son, Mirza Muhammad Ali (the eldest son of Baha'u'llah's second wife), then about forty.

Both of these sons had been loyal to their father, and were trusted by him. Abbas Effendi was appointed by

Baha'u'llah to be in charge of external affairs of the
Cause, and Mirza Muhammad Ali was given charge of
internal affairs. Baha'u'llah did not think highly of
Munira Khanum, the wife of Abbas Effendi, and perhaps it was partly for this reason that Abbas Effendi and
his wife, daughters, sister, and mother lived together in
the city of Akka, while Baha'u'llah and his other wives
and sons and the remaining members of his family lived
in the Bahji Palace several miles away. Abbas Effendi
was given the responsibility of writing the authorized
history of the Babi-Baha'i movement, which he did in
1886 as an anonymous work entitled *A Traveller's Narrative*. He procured the property on Mt. Carmel near Haifa
on which, as a result of his efforts, the mausoleum for
the Bab was later built. Mirza Muhammad Ali was also
given great responsibility. Baha'u'llah dictated his Epistles to him, and entrusted him with all the sacred writings. He was also given the authority to revise — with
the help of a trusted believer — and publish several of
Baha'u'llah's books, including the *Aqdas*. This was done
in Bombay in 1890, two years before the death of his
father, and there is no evidence that Baha'u'llah expressed any dissatisfaction with the services rendered by
his son.

When the Bab chose Mirza Yahya as his successor
and gave him high titles, he appointed one whom he had
never seen, and some might later have said that this was
a mistake. However, such a criticism could not be made
of Baha'u'llah, for he chose his own sons, men known and
trusted not only by him but by all the Baha'is. And to
prevent the kind of schism which had occurred between
him and Subh-i-Azal, he made the appointment quite
definite and clear in his Will. In this document the
father, no doubt realizing that trouble was brewing and
might erupt after his death, pleads with all members of
his family and all believers to love and honor the

Branches and to love one another and live in peace. "The creed of God is for love and union," he says,

> make it not the cause of discord and disunion. . . .
> He hath forbidden disputes and strife with an
> absolute prohibition in the book [Aqdas]. This is
> the command of God in this Greatest Manifesta-
> tion. . . . O My Branches, My Twigs and My Rela-
> tions! Make not the course of order to be the cause
> of confusion. . . . Respect and regard for the
> Branches is incumbent upon all.

Unfortunately, these pleas for harmony fell on deaf ears. The sad story of the events that followed the death of Baha'u'llah is related by Mirza Jawad, who had come with Baha'u'llah from Edirne, and had remained a faithful follower through the years at Akka:

> Alas, alas for what we see today! All these spir-
> itual virtues and humane practices have under-
> gone a complete change. Concord has been re-
> placed by dissension, constancy by cruelty, and
> affection by enmity. Dissent and mutual avoidance
> have appeared in this community. . . . antagonism
> and separation arose between father and son,
> brother and sister, husband and wife, and so forth;
> nay, God be our refuge! even envy and hatred.

The cause of this dissension was, according to Mirza Jawad, "the love of self and seeking after supremacy" of Abbas Effendi.

There is no question that Baha'u'llah appointed Abbas Effendi as his successor. But what authority was he to have? The Bab had indicated that his successor Subh-i-Azal had the same rank that he had, and was one with him. But Baha'u'llah made it very clear that anyone who succeeded him could never claim to share his rank as a Great Manifestation. Before his death he stated in the *Kitab-i-Aqdas*, that anyone who claims "Command," that is, claims to have the rank of a Manifestation, before a thousand years is a false liar. Hence, Abbas Effendi was

not authorized to take his father's place, and be a continuation of his Manifestation. But soon it appeared that
this was what he wanted to do. He called himself Abdu'l-
Baha (the Slave of Baha), and professed perfect submission to his father's Will. But he also assumed the title,
"the Center of the Covenant," a title which many Baha'is
thought belonged only to God. "Abbas Effendi," writes
Mirza Jawad, "after he had attained to supremacy . . .
claimed such lofty stations and high degrees as belong
exclusively to Divine Theophanies." And he quotes several pages of the new leader's sayings which show how
high Abbas Effendi's aspirations were.

One of Abbas Effendi's claims was that he alone had
the right to interpret the writings of Baha'u'llah. Though
he never called himself a new Manifestation, by this
claim, and by asserting that his writings were equally
authoritative with those of his father, he assumed a station of which Baha'u'llah would most probably have
warmly disapproved. However, it seems that most of the
Baha'is fully agreed to these claims, and were quite
ready to follow their divinely appointed leader, no matter what station he might claim for himself. But there
were a number who, like Mirza Jawad, for various reasons deeply resented the attitude and the acts of Abdu'l-
Baha, and the leader of the opposition soon came to be
Mirza Muhammad Ali, brother of Abbas Effendi, and
appointed by Baha'u'llah as the second in succession. It
seems that Muhammad Ali did not claim to be the rightful successor to his father, for he had no right to the
leadership of the Cause till Abbas should die. His protest, and that of those who joined him, was against the
claims of the "Center of the Covenant" to absolute
authority. He and his party called themselves "Unitarians"; they were stigmatized by Abdu'l-Baha and his
followers as "Violators of the Covenant."

The strife waxed fierce, and unseemly things were
said and done by both sides. The Unitarians sought a

conference with the party of Abdu'l-Baha that they might refer the matter to the writings of Baha'u'llah, as had been commanded in the *Kitab-i-Aqdas,* but Abdu'l-Baha did not reply to their frequent requests, and the conference was never held. It seems that almost all of the members of the family of Baha'u'llah sided with Mirza Muhammad Ali and the Unitarians.

Abdu'l-Baha accordingly took disciplinary action. He not only excommunicated all of his relatives who opposed him, but later deprived them of the allowances which Baha'u'llah had previously given them from the funds that came to him from the believers in Iran and other lands.

The controversy between the two factions grew increasingly bitter and continued for years. The Unitarians accused Abbas Effendi of appropriating to himself "covenants and promises referring exclusively to previous and future Theophanies." When one of the oldest and most respected disciples of Baha'u'llah, who had been his life-long amanuensis, made this accusation, Abbas Effendi, according to Mirza Jawad, appeared on the scene, seized the old man by the hand, and "expelled him from the house bareheaded and barefooted, while his followers beat him on the head and face." Paying no attention to his protests, they dragged him to the tomb of Baha'u'llah, "where Abbas Effendi struck him with his hand a painful blow," after which he was imprisoned in a stable. Later, after being released, he went to the house of Abbas Effendi in Akka, hoping to have a conference with him about the situation, but he was refused admittance, and was finally handed over to the police. Four years later he died, and all the relics and writings of Baha'u'llah which were in his possession were taken away by night by Abbas Effendi.

Those defending Abbas Effendi claimed that the true ground of this crisis was Mirza Muhammad Ali's jealousy and envy of his brother. The language of both sides was full of vituperation and insult. Muhammad Ali and his followers were accused of stealing sacred writings and even of conspiring to murder Abdu'l-Baha. Yet the men who brought such grievous accusations against one another were brothers, both sons of Baha'u'llah, both Most Great Branches from the ancient Stock, both chosen by their father to be in turn his successors, and both enjoined to honor and love one another in their father's Will.

While these unhappy events were taking place in Akka, the first Baha'i missionary to America was busily engaged in preaching and making converts in the West. We shall tell of his activities in the next chapter. Meanwhile, Abbas Effendi continued to live and worship as a Muslim, saying the Muslim prayers and keeping the Fast of Ramazan, just as his father had done. And the marriages and funerals in the family were all conducted by the Muslim religious leaders according to the Muslim rites.

Abdu'l-Baha was without doubt a man of great ability and possessed a commanding personality. While he was warmly hated by the "Covenant-breakers" he was literally adored by some of the new converts who began coming from America to visit "The Master" in Akka. One of them, Mr. Horace Holley, who became one of the outstanding Baha'i leaders in America, and edited *Bahai Scriptures,* speaks thus of his feelings on meeting Abdu'l-Baha:

> He displayed a beauty of stature, an inevitable harmony of attitude and dress I had never seen or thought of in men. Without ever having visualized the Master, I knew that this was he. . . . My heart leaped, and my knees weakened, a thrill of acute, receptive feeling flowed from head to foot. . . . From sheer happiness I wanted to cry. . . . While my own personality was flowing away . . . a new being, not my own, assumed its place. A glory, as it were, from the summits of human nature poured into me.

. . . In Abdu'l-Baha I felt the awful presence of Baha'u'llah, and . . . I realized that I had thus drawn as near as man now may to pure spirit and pure being.

When Baha'u'llah and his followers were sent to Akka as political prisoners in 1868 they were for some time confined to the city, but after several years they were given considerable liberty of movement, and were allowed to travel to other parts of the country. Then, because of the activities of the Baha'is and the strife which we have described, the Ottoman government sent a commssion to investigate the situation, and as a result of its report the freedom which they had enjoyed for more than twenty years was taken from them, and they were once more confined to the city of Akka. This occurred in 1901. Abdu'l-Baha placed the entire blame for this unfortunate occurrence on his brother Mirza Muhammad, whom he charged with giving false information to the Turkish authorities. This restriction was continued till the Turkish Revolution of 1908 when all political prisoners were set free. Thereafter, the Baha'is could go anywhere they wished.

Much of Abdu'l-Baha's time was spent in writing, for he, like his father, carried on a large correspondence with believers in Iran and in other lands, and his Tablets were as highly esteemed as had been those of Baha'u'llah. By the strength of his personality and the remarkable influence which he exercised over his followers, he was able to draw the great majority of the Baha'is of the world after him; the Unitarians never became a strong party and gradually disappeared from the scene. After the travel restrictions were removed, Abdu'l-Baha made a journey to Europe and Egypt in 1911. The next year he sailed for America, where he remained for seven months, and on the return journey again visited Europe, Great Britain, and Egypt.

During the eight years that followed these journeys

Abdu'l-Baha remained in Haifa, which is near Akka. At the time of the First World War (1914-1918) he is said to have done much for the relief of the famine-stricken people about him, and to have been most generous in giving to the poor from his own provisions. Finally, Haifa fell into the hands of the British, and Turkish rule came to an end on September 23, 1918.

Mr. J. E. Esselmont spent two and a half months as the guest of Abdu'l-Baha in Haifa during 1919-20, and published his experiences in a book *Baha'u'llah and the New Era*. He wrote:

> From the beginning of the British occupation, large numbers of soldiers and Government officials of all ranks, even the highest, sought interviews with Abdu'l-Baha. . . . So profoundly impressed were the Government representatives by his noble character and his great work in the interests of peace, conciliation, and the true prosperity of the people, that a knighthood of the British Empire was conferred on Abdu'l-Baha, the ceremony taking place in the garden of the Military Governor of Haifa on the 27th day of April, 1920.

Thus the Center of the Covenant became "Sir Abdu'l-Baha Abbas, K.B.E."

In the same book Mr. Esselmont described his host as follows:

> At that time, although nearly seventy-six years of age, he was still remarkably vigorous, and accomplished daily an almost incredible amount of work. Although often very weary he showed wonderful powers of recuperation. . . . His unfailing patience, gentleness, kindliness and tact made his presence like a benediction. . . . Both at lunch and supper he used to entertain a number of pilgrims and friends, and charm his guests with happy and humorous stories. . . . "My house is the home of laughter and mirth," he declared, and indeed it was

so. He delighted in gathering together people of various races, colours, nations and religions in unity and cordial friendship around his hospitable board.

On Friday, November 25, 1921, Abdu'l-Baha attended the noonday Muslim prayer at the Mosque in Haifa, and afterwards distributed alms to the poor with his own hands, as was his wont. Less than three days later he died. The following day the funeral services were conducted by the Muslim clergy, and a very large number of people from various religions attended, along with the British High Commissioner and other officials of the Government. Nine representatives from the Muslim, Christian, and Jewish communities spoke in praise of the deceased, and then the body was carried to Mt. Carmel and buried in the mausoleum of the Bab. His grave became a place of pilgrimage for Baha'is.

9

The Baha'i Faith Goes
West and East

SINCE THE SEVENTH CENTURY, when the followers of Muhammad set forth to make Islam the religion of the world, no new religion born in the Near East had attempted to become a universal religion till Baha'i missionaries, less than a century ago, undertook to convert not only the peoples of the East but also of the West to their faith. In this chapter we will tell the interesting story of the establishment of the Baha'i Cause in America, and in other distant lands.

The first Baha'i missionary to America was Dr. Ibrahim George Kheiralla (Khayru'llah), a native of Lebanon, and a graduate (1870) of the American College which had been founded by Protestant missionaries in Beirut. Dr. Kheiralla was born in a Chaldean family in 1849, the year before the death of the Bab in Iran. It was said by one who knew him well that he was a teacher, a healer of nervous diseases, a writer, a trader, and "pretty much everything else." Because of his irregular conduct he was rejected by the Christian community in his native land. He was "a man of strong mind, acute argumentative faculties, fine conversational powers and altogether an interesting personality."

In 1872, four years after the arrival of Baha'u'llah in Akka, Kheiralla went from Lebanon to Egypt, where he

engaged in trade for twenty-one years. There in 1890 he
was converted to the Baha'i faith. In reply to a letter
which he wrote to Baha'u'llah, he received a Tablet from
his Master. Soon after the death of Baha'u'llah in 1892,
Dr. Kheiralla went to Russia on personal business, travelled from there to Europe, and thence to America, where
he arrived in December. He at once began to tell the
Good News of "the Appearance of the Father and the
establishment of His Kingdom on earth," and it was
through his tireless efforts that the Baha'i Cause was
first established in the New World. After spending some
time in New York and Michigan, Dr. Kheiralla went to
Chicago in February, 1894, and established his center
there. In the Congress of Religions which was held in
connection with the Chicago Exposition in 1893, the Babi-
Baha'i Movement had received favorable notice, and
there were numerous people in and about Chicago who
were eager to learn more about this new religion from
the East.

After having made many converts, Dr. Kheiralla
wrote to Abdu'l-Baha to report his success. When his
Greek wife who had remained in Cairo refused to join
him he divorced her, and in 1895 married an English
woman. With her he made a journey to England, and
then returned to Chicago, "where he applied himself
day and night, without wearying, to teaching the people."
In Kenosha, fifty miles from Chicago, he met with great
success.

Dr. Kheiralla taught inquirers in private lessons. He
began with thirteen lectures, and one inquirer took careful notes which were later published. The first ten lectures had little to do with the Baha'i faith, and dealt
with metaphysics, dreams, numbers, allegorical interpretations of the Bible, prayer, and so on. But the intense
curiosity of the hearers was aroused by the promise of
the revelation of some mystery in the eleventh lesson.
Accordingly, the appearance of the Bab, Baha'u'llah and

Abdu'l-Baha was proclaimed in that lecture. The Bab had announced that the Father had come, and the Father was Baha'u'llah. Abdu'l-Baha was Jesus Christ, the Son of God. The Millennium, said Dr. Kheiralla, would come in 1917, when one third of the people of the world would become Baha'is. He stated that there were at that time (1898) fifty-five million Baha'is in the world. He interpreted all the prophecies in the book of Daniel and the Revelation as applying to Baha'u'llah, in order to convince Christians that his coming had been foretold in their Bible. "We have been taught nothing about the life and character of Baha," wrote one listener, "no ethics, no religious life, does he pretend to teach."

Only persons who were willing to write a letter to Abdu'l-Baha, professing faith in him, were permitted to attend more than thirteen lectures. The letter given to the students to sign and send reads in part:

> To the Greatest Branch,
>
> In God's Name, the Greatest Branch, I humbly confess the oneness and singleness of Almighty God, my Creator, and I believe in His appearance in the human form; I believe in His establishing His holy household; in His departure, and that He has delivered His kingdom to Thee, O Greatest Branch, His dearest son and mystery. I beg that I may be accepted in this glorious kingdom and that my name may be registered in the "Book of Believers". . . .
>
> Most humbly thy servant. . . .

Great spiritual gifts were promised to those who wrote the letter.

In the summer of 1898 Dr. and Mrs. Kheiralla participated in a pilgrimage to Akka. As they passed through England and France, Dr. Kheiralla gave the "Most Great Name" to a number of believers, thus establishing the Baha'i faith in Europe. After visiting Egypt, the sixteen members of the party arrived in Akka in December, and a representative of Abdu'l-Baha welcomed them there. Abdu'l-Baha himself cordially greeted Dr. Kheiralla in his own home, kissing him, and saying, "Welcome to thee, O Baha's Peter, O second Columbus, Conqueror of America!" Abdu'l-Baha had a fez put on Dr. Kheiralla's head as a mark of special honor, and took him to the tomb of Baha'u'llah, telling him that he was the first pilgrim to whom the door of this chamber had been opened for prayer. Dr. Kheiralla also joined Abdu'l-Baha in breaking ground for the Mausoleum on Mt. Carmel, which Abdu'l-Baha was about to build for the body of the Bab soon to be brought from Iran. "This is an honor which none of the believers except thee has enjoyed," Abdu'l-Baha told him. And he gave Dr. Kheiralla the title of "Shepherd of God's flocks in America."

Before long, however, difficulties arose. Dr. Kheiralla was eager to explain his teaching to his Master, and to discuss questions of theology with him, but Abdu'l-Baha was not inclined to answer questions and was displeased when his missionary differed with him. Dr. Kheiralla wanted copies of books by Baha'u'llah which he did not possess, but Abdu'l-Baha would not give them to him, even denying their existence, and Dr. Kheiralla had to acquire them later in Egypt. Moreover, none of the pilgrims was permitted to see either any members of the family of Baha'u'llah, except Abdu'l-Baha's sister, or any followers of Mirza Muhammad Ali, though they learned of the serious split in the family. Dr. Kheiralla stayed six months, long enough to understand fully what was going on. Meanwhile, two of the Americans accused Dr. Kheiralla of immoral conduct. Abdu'l-Baha heard the stories and repeated them to the missionary's wife; on their return to Egypt she left her husband. So the pilgrimage was not an altogether happy experience.

After returning to America Dr. Kheiralla became increasingly estranged from Abdu'l-Baha. As he studied the *Kitab-i-Aqdas* and Baha'u'llah's other writings, he

became convinced that the claims which Abdu'l-Baha
made for himself were unjustified. From Abdu'l-Baha's
conduct and correspondence Dr. Kheiralla concluded that
he was double-faced in his dealings, and was promoting
discord rather than harmony and love among believers.
So after seven months Dr. Kheiralla broke with Abbas
Effendi and went over to the party of Mirza Muhammad
Ali. At the same time the devotees of Abbas Effendi in
America rejected Dr. Kheiralla, maintaining that his
teachings were erroneous and his conduct immoral. Dr.
Kheiralla responded with counter charges, and the Chicago and Kenosha assemblies were rent asunder. Several
hundred believers sided with Dr. Kheiralla, and became
known as "Behaists," but the majority, who called themselves "Baha'is," remained faithful to Abdu'l-Baha.

In 1900 and the years following, Abdu'l-Baha sent a
succession of learned and experienced Baha'i missionaries to America to bring back the lost sheep. On the
whole they failed, though they made some new converts.
The quarrel resulted in many believers deserting the
Cause. According to the U.S. Census of 1906, the Behaists
had dwindled to forty, and the Baha'is had increased
to 1280. Both sides wrote books and pamphlets stating
their own case and denouncing their rivals. The spirit
of love and forgiveness was noticeably absent from these
polemics.

During the missionary period summarized in the last
few pages, the American press publicized the apparent
spread of the Baha'i cause in the West, and no doubt
many readers were amazed at what they read. For example, the front page of the *New York Herald* of August
12, 1900, was adorned with pictures of Akka and of Abbas
Effendi, and bore the headlines: "These Believe that
Christ has Returned to Earth" — "Strange Faith has
Attracted Many Followers" — "A New Gospel According to Abbas of Acre." The article begins: "Is Christ
living in the world today? There are tens of thousands

of persons who believe that He is. . . . There are hundreds
who claim to have looked upon the face and to have
listened to the voice of the Divinity." Other newspapers
printed similar stories, stressing the oriental robes of
the missionaries and the obvious wealth of those who
attended the meetings.

In spite of such publicity and exaggerated claims as
to the number of converts, the Baha'i Cause suffered
greatly from internal strife and made little progress in
America till the visit of Abdu'l-Baha himself in 1912.
After the Turkish Revolution in 1908 the "prisoners" in
Akka were free to travel wherever they wished, and
Abdu'l-Baha soon took advantage of his liberty to visit
the lands in the West where his zealous missionaries
had prepared the way for him. It is noteworthy that he
did not go to Iran, the land of his birth, where the great
majority of Baha'is then lived. His first long journey out
of Akka, where he had lived for forty-three years, was
to France and England in 1911. He spent some time in
London and Paris, meeting believers and inquirers, and
giving many addresses. On the return journey he visited
Egypt, then under British rule, where many Iranian
Baha'is had gone seeking freedom and business.

This tour proved so rewarding that in the spring of
1912 Abdu'l-Baha, no doubt at the invitation and expense
of the believers in America, set forth on a journey which
lasted nearly two years. His coming had been prepared
for long in advance by attractive publicity. The *New
York Times,* on July 2, 1911, published a full-page article
entitled "Bahaism, Founded in Martyrdom, Taking Root
Here." In large letters it stated that "Though This Persian Religion Was Established Only Seventy Years Ago,
Its Followers Have Suffered Persecutions Rivaling Those
of the Early Christians—Now Numbers 10,000,000 Adherents." There were pictures of Abdu'l-Baha, of a group
of bearded and turbaned Baha'i leaders, of "the prison
in which Baha Ullah wrote many of his books," as well

as of his house in Akka, and his tomb. The article played up the persecutions which the Baha'is had endured, stating that there were ten thousand, and according to some, thirty thousand martyrs in Iran in the years 1848-1852. It was not explained that those who died were not Baha'is but Babis. The actual number of Babis killed in the several insurrections during this period was in fact less than five thousand. "The sect inculcates," said the article, "a love of the world rather than of country, and declares all religions to be equally true." It is clear that the author of the article possessed more literary skill than knowledge of the history of the Babi-Baha'i Movement.

When Abdu'l-Baha arrived in New York a woman reporter interviewed him, and her story appeared as a full-page article in the *New York Times* of April 21, 1912, under the heading: "A Message From Abdul Baha, Head of the Bahais." The article begins:

> Within the last week there has come to New York an old man with a worn and beautiful face, who wears a long brown gown and a white turban, and speaks the strange-sounding guttural language of Persia. On the pier he was welcomed by hundreds of people, for he is Abdul Baha, or "The Servant of God," the head of the Bahaist movement, and he is known to tens of thousands of followers all over the world as the "Master." For forty years he had been in prison, and his father, the former head of the Bahaists, died in prison. . . . They preached the love of God and the brotherhood of man, and for this the Persian Government exiled and the Turkish Government imprisoned them.

After giving the orthodox Baha'i account of the history of the Cause, the reporter describes her interview with the Master. She found the reception room in his apartment filled with flowers.

> A rather small man with a white beard and the kindest and gentlest face in the world held out a

hand. In his brown habit he was extraordinarily picturesque, but one did not think of that, for he smiled a charming smile, and walking before and holding his visitor's hand, he led her to a chair.

Evidently the Master was as happy to meet the reporter as she was to meet him. In fact, he told her so. He gave his visitor a rose as she was departing, patted her on the shoulder, and spoke to her in Persian. His interpreter· said, "He says he is pleased with you." Nor was she the only one whose heart was won by this picturesque and kind old man. One of the American Baha'is told the reporter, "For that man I'd jump head first from a fifteenth story window." And the reporter added, "So it is with everybody who has come in contact with Abdu'l-Baha."

From this auspicious beginning, Abdu'l-Baha's triumphal tour took him to many parts of America. He addressed the Persian-American Educational Society, an organization operated by Baha'is, in Washington on April 20. On May 1 (during the Rizwan Feast) Abdu'l-Baha was present for the dedication of the grounds on which the famous Mashriqu'l-Adhkar was to be built in Wilmette, Illinois. A five acre site north of Chicago near the shore of Lake Michigan had been purchased, and

> Abdu'l-Baha, using a golden trowel, broke ground, and others of the different races who were present used picks and shovels and prepared a place into which Abdu'l-Baha put a stone. He said: "The mystery of this building is great. It cannot be unveiled yet, but its erection is the most important undertaking of this day. This temple of God in Chicago will be to the spiritual body of the world what the inrush of the spirit is to the physical body of man."

The plans for the temple were elaborate, and the money came in slowly, but it was at last finished and dedicated on May 2, 1953. Could the Master have seen the realization of his dreams he would no doubt have been very happy.

On December 5, 1912, after a busy and successful seven months' tour in America, Abdu'l-Baha sailed from New York for Great Britain. He remained there for six weeks, visiting various cities, encouraging believers, giving addresses as before, and receiving many notables. He then spent two months in Paris, after which he visited Germany and Austria. Finally, he resided for six months in Egypt, and reached Akka on December 5, 1913, after an absence of twenty months, having completed a tour both pleasant for himself and profitable to the Cause.

Since the story of the introduction of the Baha'i Faith to America has been told at some length, no attempt will be made to give a detailed account of the spread of the movement in Great Britain and Europe. As we have already noted, both Abdu'l-Baha and his missionaries visited the various countries, spoke in churches and before all sorts of gatherings, met inquirers, and established Baha'i groups, as they had done west of the Atlantic. Some of the writings of Baha'u'llah and Abdu'l-Baha were translated and published in English and French and German. After his return to Akka, Abdu'l-Baha directed an "unceasing flow of His Tablets" to the scattered groups of believers.

Converts to the Baha'i Cause were not only being made in the West. Zealous believers were also busily engaged in the East, telling the Good News of Baha'u'llah. Two "teachers," presumably American Baha'is, went to Japan in 1914 and established meetings in Tokyo. Some young people there who were dissatisfied with other religions accepted the Baha'i Message. A number of Baha'i books were translated into Japanese and published, and many newspaper articles appeared. During the last years of his life Abdu'l-Baha addressed nineteen Tablets to people in Japan, and the Baha'i Message was taken from

Japan to Korea in 1921. The number of converts in Japan and Korea at that time is not known, but it was not great.

Many Iranians had left their country to trade or reside in India, and Baha'is soon found that India, which was under British rule, was a field in which they could labor with a freedom they did not enjoy anywhere in the Near East. There they published a monthly magazine in English, Persian, and Burmese, and there the *Kitab-i-Aqdas,* the *Iqan,* and other important Baha'i books were published in 1890 and brought back to Akka. But while some Indian natives may have been converted, it is evident from a photograph of "Representative Baha'is of India" in the *Baha'i World* that most of the believers were Iranians, not Indians. The Baha'i Message was also taken to Australia and New Zealand by American believers.

In parts of the Near East where most of the population were Sunnite Muslims, and where there was little or no freedom of religion, there were few Baha'is who were not Iranians. One of the largest groups of believers outside Iran was found in Egypt, where many Iranians resided, and where, under British rule, Baha'is were able to publish books and carry on other activities which were not possible in lands ruled by Turkey.

Naturally, during this period the largest number of Baha'is lived in the land of Baha'u'llah's birth. There were Baha'is in all the larger cities and towns and in many villages, but since no census was ever taken, it is impossible to accurately estimate their numbers. Following the example of their leaders in Akka, they usually conformed to the religious practices of their Shi'ite Muslim neighbors and seldom professed their Baha'i faith openly. However, more or less secret meetings were held in homes, and tactful but effective missionary work was carried on by a number of able apostles, as well as by many of the faithful, both men and women. Books were prepared and printed outside Iran, or secretly published in Iran, containing detailed instructions for presenting the Baha'i Message to Muslims, Jews, Christians, and Zoroastrians, and for answering the objections of these unbelievers. Muslims, a number of Jews, and a few Zoroastrians were converted. However, while new converts were being made, many who once professed faith fell away, and it is probable that the number of Baha'is in Iran was less in 1921 than it was in 1892.

As has been said, the government of Iran recognized four religions, Zoroastrianism, Judaism, Christianity, and Islam, and allowed the three minority groups to worship and conduct their affairs according to the laws of their religions. Though the Baha'is outnumbered the Zoroastrians, and claimed to be more numerous than the Iranian Jews and Christians, they were not recognized as a separate religious community, but were counted as Muslims, and were seldom persecuted by the government. However, when the Baha'is became too aggressive in propagating their religion, they sometimes stirred up fanatical opposition by the Muslims, and this occasionally resulted in riots and murders. The worst of these occurred in Yazd and Isfahan in 1903 when a hundred people were said to have been killed. However, not all the unfortunate people counted as "martyrs" were Baha'is, for it sometimes happened that a person who wished to get rid of an enemy or a creditor would brand him a Baha'i, and would then incite the Muslim clergy or the authorities to kill him for being an infidel. The total number of Baha'i martyrs in Iran during the rule of Abdu'l-Baha has been given by one authority as twenty-five and by another as about one hundred. The usually tolerant attitude of the Iranian government is indicated by the fact that many Baha'is were employed in the Post Office and the Customs and in other government offices. There was, however, usually less freedom in the provinces than in the capital.

The Iranian Baha'is were fairly numerous and some

of them had wealth, but they did very little as a group to minister to the sick and poor and uneducated portion of the population of their country, though it was commonly reported that they were often ready to find jobs for people whom they were trying to convert. There were several good schools in Teheran and other places which were established by Western Baha'is, and for a time a small medical work was carried on by foreigners, not by the Iranian believers.

Baha'is in Iran differed little from their Muslim neighbors. Outwardly they wore the same clothes, and their women usually appeared in public covered by the sort of veils used by Muslims. Nor were their characters and morals different. They sometimes practiced polygamy. They usually practiced *taqiya* (concealment of religious belief), and this often led to lying about their religion, and to untruthfulness and dishonesty in general. Though there were of course exceptions, Iranian Baha'is on the whole were not at the time of Abdu'l-Baha conspicuous for the virtues of purity, honesty, truthfulness, love, and service to others which their leaders in Akka had enjoined on them. Of their devotion to Abdu'l-Baha there was no question, but like some adherents to other religions they often failed to demonstrate their faith in their daily lives.

Before the death of Abdu'l-Baha, his Cause had been carried to many lands, both East and West, but the number of Baha'is in all the world was still comparatively small, probably less than fifty thousand.

10

The Teachings of Abdu'l-Baha

WHEN ABBAS EFFENDI was a child his father Baha was an ardent disciple of the Bab. The Bab was executed when Abbas was nine years old, and from that time till he reached the age of twenty-five, he, like his father, was obedient to Subh-i-Azal, his uncle, the successor to the Bab. In 1866 when his father Baha claimed to be a new Manifestation, Abbas Effendi became a Baha'i. His beliefs, therefore, were first those of the People of the *Bayan,* and later those inculcated by his father Baha'u'llah. As long as his father lived, Abbas Effendi followed his teachings faithfully. As a Babi he had believed the doctrine that God is unknowable except in his Manifestations, who are one with his Will. These Manifestations, who appeared at intervals of about one thousand years, were, according to the doctrine of the Bab and Baha'u'llah, the same as the Great Prophets of Islam — Adam, Noah, Abraham, Moses, Jesus, and Muhammad. To these. the Babis added Ali Muhammad the Bab, whom they considered the greatest of the Manifestations to appear so far. This was undoubtedly the belief of Abbas Effendi before he became a Baha'i. But when he became a Baha'i he professed faith in his father as the greatest of the Manifestations, relegated the Bab to the position of Forerunner for Baha'u'llah, and portrayed Subh-i-Azal as the arch-enemy of the Cause of God.

When Baha'u'llah died in 1892 and Abbas Effendi became, in accordance with his father's Will, the divinely appointed head of the Baha'i community, the first problem which faced him was that of his own position and authority. In his Will, as well as in the *Kitab-i-Aqdas,* Baha'u'llah had commanded all believers to honor and obey the Branches, especially the two eldest who were to succeed him in turn. Baha'u'llah had been a Manifestation, and he spoke as God. But how would his successor speak, and how much authority would he have? Baha'u'llah had made it quite clear that his son could not follow his example and claim to be a Manifestation, for in the *Kitab-i-Aqdas* he had stated, "Whoever claims Command before the completion of a thousand years is a false liar. . . . Whoever explains this verse or interprets it in any other way than that plainly sent down, he will be deprived of the Spirit and Mercy of God. . . ." However, he also commanded that after his death all matters which his followers did not understand in the *Aqdas* were to be referred to the Branch. But would the interpretations of the Book by the Branch be infallible? And would the decisions and pronouncements of the Branch be absolutely authoritative, as were those of Baha'u'llah?

As we have seen, Abbas Effendi gave to himself the title "Abdu'l-Baha" (The Slave of Baha) to indicate his complete submission to his father. But he also claimed for himself the sole right to interpret the writings of Baha'u'llah, and called himself the Center of the Covenant.

As was recorded in Chapter 8, when Abbas Effendi began to exercise this authority, a number of his father's old, devoted, and prominent followers became disaffected and left him. However, as his appointment to be the first successor to Baha'u'llah could not be questioned by anyone, the majority of Baha'is readily gave him the same reverence and devotion that they had given to his father, and received and cherished his Tablets as inspired and infallible pronouncements. Abdu'l-Baha became to them not so much a new Manifestation as an extension of Baha'u'llah. The death of the father probably made little difference to the believers in Iran and other lands, because his son, the Most Mighty Branch, did all for them that Baha'u'llah had done.

In 1866 when Baha'u'llah took over the leadership of the Babi movement and undertook to lead the Babis forward, he made certain changes in the laws given by the Bab, claiming that he was himself a new lawgiver sent by God. When his son Abdu'l-Baha assumed the leadership of the Baha'i community, he realized that his father's changes were not drastic enough, and that still more reforms had to be made if the religion were to survive and expand. Since Abdu'l-Baha was not a Manifestation he could not abrogate the laws of Baha'u'llah and give new ones in their place, so it was necessary for him to content himself with being an Interpreter and changing impractical regulations with his infallible interpretation. This he did as occasion arose.

For example, the only limitations which Baha'u'llah places on marriage in the *Kitab-i-Aqdas* are that a man may not marry more than two women at the same time, and that a son may not marry his father's wives. To Abdu'l-Baha this second provision seemed to give a man too much latitude, so he declared "that this does not mean that he is free to marry any other woman, but that the more distant the relationship between a man and a woman the better it is." Thus the divine laws were made to conform to the opinions and customs of the twentieth century, into which Abdu'l-Baha was introducing the Baha'i Cause.

When the Center of the Covenant began to turn his attention toward the West he found the need to modify Baha'u'llah's teaching even more pronounced; it became necessary for him to adjust Baha'i doctrine to the beliefs of people who had been influenced by Christian or Western concepts. So, as an observer in nearby Beirut has stated, Abbas Effendi presented one face to the East and quite a different face to the Europeans and Americans who visited him in Akka and whom he later visited in their own lands. Both the Bab and Baha'u'llah had read the Bible, and the writings of both were somewhat influenced by Biblical teachings. However, both sowed their seed chiefly in Islamic soil, and they did not grapple with the problem of presenting their doctrines to people who called God "Father" and who considered Jesus to be the Son and perfect revealer of God. Dr. Kheiralla, himself from a Christian background, sought to make Baha'ism intelligible and attractive to Americans. He largely ignored Muhammad, who was never greatly admired by Christians either in the West or in the East. He introduced Baha'u'llah as the Manifestation of God the Father, and therefore greater than Jesus Christ the Son of God. And who was Abdu'l-Baha? He was Christ come again, as he had promised! So the American converts came to Akka to see Christ, and some of them worshipped him as "Master."

However, after Abdu'l-Baha's visits to the West it appears that he found these high titles and the worship which some gave to him a cause of embarrassment, and in 1914 he expressed himself quite strongly about his position. He said:

> I am Abdul Baha, and no more. I am not pleased with whoever praises me with any other title. I am the Servant at the threshold of the Blessed Perfection. . . . Whoever mentions any other name save this will not please me at all. . . . After the Departure of the Blessed Perfection and until the Appearance of the next Manifestation there is no other station save the *Station of Servitude*, pure and absolute.

And at another time he stated: "I am not Christ, I am

not Eternal God, I am but the servant of Baha." However, many Baha'is still thought him to be one with his father in power and glory, and his writings were included with those of Baha'u'llah in their sacred Scriptures. Thus the editors, in the "Foreword to the Excerpts from the Will of Abdu'l-Baha," published in the *Baha'i World*, write:

> By the appointment of Abdu'l-Baha as the Center of His Covenant, Baha'u'llah prolonged His own ministry for wellnigh thirty years. . . . For the words of Abdu'l-Baha, according to the text of this appointment, have equal rank and spiritual validity with those of the Manifestation [i.e., Baha'u'llah].

We may, therefore, conclude that in the West as well as in the East Abdu'l-Baha was widely thought of as a divine being, a continuation of the Manifestation of Baha'u'llah.

The followers of Abdu'l-Baha consider all that he wrote and spoke to be inspired and infallible teaching. Since he spoke and wrote a very great deal between 1892 and 1921, it is impossible to give more than a few samples of his precepts and pronouncements in this chapter.

Abdu'l-Baha taught that Baha'u'llah is God Manifest. "This is the day in which the Lord of Hosts has come down from heaven on the clouds of glory." Baha'u'llah is the greatest of the Manifestations and was foretold in all the previous Scriptures. It is noteworthy that Abdu'l-Baha, even in America and England, did not often speak of God as "Father." One reason was probably that he, coming from a Muslim tradition in which it was considered blasphemous to call God "Father" and Jesus "Son of God," found it difficult to use these terms. Moreover, according to his belief, God is impersonal and unknowable. If God does not possess personality, it would be impossible to address him as "Father," or to address him at all. So Abdu'l-Baha usually followed the Islamic custom of calling him "Lord," and of speaking of believers not as "children of God," but as God's "slaves," translated "servants" in English. Even the eldest son of Baha'u'llah the Lord took as his title the "Slave of Baha."

Muslims have often accused Christians of corrupting their Scriptures, and have said that the Bible is no longer authentic. Baha'u'llah pronounced this charge false, and both he and his son frequently referred to the Bible as a proof of their doctrines. However, when the Bible teaching did not agree with Baha'i ideas, it was often interpreted in such a way as to change the meaning completely. For instance, all miraculous events like the healing of the sick and the resurrection of Christ were said to have only a spiritual meaning.

Abdu'l-Baha declared that all the holy Manifestations were united and agreed in purpose and teaching, and he named Zoroaster and Buddha among the traditional Manifestations. "There is no differentiation possible," he continued, "in their mission and teachings; all are reflectors of reality. . . . and reality is not multiple; it is one." Therefore, he says, "When Christians act according to the teachings of Christ they are called Baha'is. For the foundations of Christianity and the religion of Baha are one." Hence, all the great religions are true, and all followers of these faiths can and should unite in one world faith, namely, the Baha'i Faith.

This teaching was pleasing to people in the West who resented the exclusive claims of both Christianity and Islam. It was quite easy for members of the Christian community with only a superficial acquaintance with Christianity and other religions to assent to the proposition that all religions are one. Whether a Jew could remain a member of the synagogue, or a Christian a member of a church, upon becoming a Baha'i, was never answered clearly by Abdu'l-Baha. However, since he

attended the Muslim mosque and observed the rites of
Islam in Akka, and was recognized by Muslims as one
of them, the conclusion could easily be drawn that such
dual membership by Baha'is was possible and desirable.

From the New Testament Abdu'l-Baha learned the
primary importance of love, and love for all men occupied a large place in his teaching. In writing about love
he says:

> Let us have love, and more love, a love that melts
> all opposition, that sweeps away all barriers, that
> conquers all foes, a love that aboundeth in charity.
> . . . Each one must be a sign of love, a center of
> love, a sun of love. . . . a universe of love. Hast thou
> love? Then thy power is irresistible.

And again:

> You must love humanity in order to uplift and beau-
> tify humanity. Even if people slay you, yet you must
> love them. . . . We are creatures of the same God,
> therefore we must love all as children of God even
> though they are doing us harm. Christ loved his
> persecutors. It is possible for us to attain to that
> love.

After reading these beautiful words it is disappointing
to discover from other utterances of Abdu'l-Baha that
he found it impossible to love certain people. It appears
that to the end of his life he cherished great bitterness
toward the "Covenant-breakers," the leader of whom
was his own brother Mirza Muhammad Ali. In his Will
he speaks of them as "ferocious lions, ravening wolves,
blood-thirsty beasts," and there is no evidence that he
ever forgave and showed love to them.

In his addresses and epistles to people in the West,
Abdu'l-Baha said little about the Manifestation who followed Christ — according to the Bab and Baha'u'llah a
Manifestation superior to Christ — for he knew that
people acquainted with the Bible and the Koran would

not readily agree that Muhammad occupied a higher place than Christ, and that the teachings of the Koran were superior to those of the Sermon on the Mount. Usually he by-passed Islam, and spoke of Baha'u'llah as the Manifestation after Christ, or the return of Christ.

It is evident from his teachings that Abdu'l-Baha was not so much concerned about man's relation to God as he was about the problems of man's life on earth. "In short," he wrote, "by religion we mean those necessary bonds which unify the world of humanity." And again, "All the religions are revealed for the sake of good fellowship. The fundamentals, the foundations, of all are fellowship, unity and love." And so he spoke much about the unity of all mankind.

It is unfortunate that some of the public pronouncements of Abdu'l-Baha were marred by inaccuracies which have found their way into the *Bahai Scriptures*. For example, he said: "The Blessed Perfection Baha'u'llah belonged to the royal family of Persia." But it is well known that Baha'u'llah was not a prince. He also said: "The Blessed Perfection was a prisoner twenty-five years. During all this time he was subjected to the indignities and revilement of the people. He was persecuted, mocked and put in chains." And again:

> After twenty-four years in the greatest prison, Acca, His life was ended in great trouble and hardship. In short, all the time of the sojourn of the Blessed Perfection [Baha'u'llah] . . . in this mortal world, He was either restrained with chains or kept under hanging swords, enduring the most painful afflictions.

While Baha'u'llah had many troubles, he lived the later years of his life in comfort in the Bahji Palace outside Akka, where there were no chains or swords.

These and other glaring inaccuracies suggest that the infallibility of the Interpreter did not cover details of history. It is easier to overlook such minor mistakes, how-

ever, than to excuse Abdu'l-Baha for untrue statements
such as the following:

> In the Orient the various peoples and nations were
> in a state of antagonism and strife, manifesting the
> utmost enmity and hatred toward one another.
> Darkness encompassed the world of mankind. At
> such a time as this, Baha'u'llah appeared. He re-
> moved all the imitations and prejudices which had
> caused separation and misunderstanding, and laid
> the foundation of the one religion of God. When
> this was accomplished, Mohammedans, Christians,
> Jews, Zoroastrians, Buddhists all were united in
> actual fellowship and love.

And again:

> We have for our subject the reconciliation of the
> religious systems of the world. . . . Do not question
> the practicability of this and be not astonished. It
> has been effected and accomplished in Persia [Iran].
> . . . No traces of discord or difference remain; the ut-
> most love, kindness, and unity are apparent. They
> are united and live together like a single family in
> harmony and accord. Discord and strife have passed
> away. Love and fellowship now prevail instead.

The impression which one would get from hearing these
statements about the influence of Baha'u'llah in his native land is that Baha'ism is the dominant religion in
Iran, and that because of it religious strife has disappeared. The most charitable thing that can be said is that
Abdu'l-Baha left Iran when a boy and had not seen it
since, so was quite uninformed concerning it. Baha'is
have always been a small minority in Iran, and their
presence has unfortunately created more discord than it
has produced peace.

At Clifton, England, on January 16, 1913, Abdu'l-Baha
made a memorable address in which, among other things,
he said:

> Nearly sixty years ago when the horizon of the

Orient was in a state of the utmost gloom, warfare
existed and there was enmity between the various
creeds. . . . At such a time His Highness Baha'u'llah
arose from the horizon of Persia . . . and boldly
proclaimed peace. In order to bring peace out of the
chaos, he established certain precepts or principles.

He then proceeded to enumerate and explain ten of the
"principles" of Baha'u'llah. Briefly they are as follows:
(1) the independent investigation of truth; (2) the oneness of the human race; (3) international peace; (4)
the conformity of religion to science and reason; (5) the
banishing of religious, racial, political, and patriotic prejudice; (6) the equality of men and women; (7) the working together of all classes of society in love and harmony;
(8) "the parliament of man" as a court of last appeal in
international questions; (9) universal education; and
(10) a universal language.

It is instructive to compare this list with one drawn
up by Baha'u'llah himself some twenty-three years
earlier. Most are not found in the earlier list, so it is
more accurate to attribute these ten principles to Abdu'l-
Baha himself. Most are not religious principles at all,
and could easily be adopted by Jews, Christians, and
Muslims, as well as materialists and atheists. It is indeed
remarkable how successfully Abdu'l-Baha shook off ves-
tiges of the old Babi order, and clothed his movement
in modern garments suited to a new age in order to present his cause to the West.

A brief consideration of these principles will suffice.
The independent investigation of truth was not a new
idea, for the Shi'ite theologians had long ago maintained
that personal investigation is obligatory in matters which
concern the fundamentals of religion. And the question
arises, what possibility for independent investigation remains when Abdu'l-Baha is the only authorized interpreter of the Baha'i Scriptures, and when he tells us,
"Whatever emanates from the Center of the Covenant

is right . . . while everything else is error"? Nor is the doctrine of the oneness of humanity new, either to readers of the Bible, or to Iranians who memorized in childhood the beautiful verse of the thirteenth-century poet Sa'adi, who wrote, "The children of Adam are members of one another, created from one essence."* Baha'u'llah had some time before issued pronouncements about reducing armaments because of their great expense, and had forbidden religious war. When Old Testament prophecies were interpreted as predictions of the coming of Baha'u'llah, it was easy to take the words in Micah about the time when men would beat their swords into plowshares as a promise of his "Most Great Peace."

The "conformity of religion to science and reason," on the other hand, is an entirely new idea; there is no trace of it in the teachings of Baha'u'llah. It seems to have come from France, where the Baha'i faith was introduced by Hippolyte Dreyfus, a Jewish convert, who presented the Baha'i Cause as a scientific religion in his effort to make it acceptable to the rationalistic people of France. The Muslim ancestors of the Baha'is had previously gloried in miracles, but now the miraculous became taboo, and miracles in the Scriptures were interpreted spiritually. Abdu'l-Baha welcomed this French flavoring for his Faith.

All sorts of "prejudice must be banished." This would follow from the unity of mankind. Abdu'l-Baha knew well the evil of the prejudice and hatred from which the Bab and Baha'u'llah had suffered. Hence, from personal experience he could insist on the need for the elimination of all prejudice.

As for the "equality of men and women," Baha'u'llah knew nothing of this principle, which would have seemed quite heretical to him. This new teaching em-

* *Golestan:* Book I, Story 10.

anated not from Akka but from the West. The "working together of all classes of society in love and harmony" is a beautiful ideal, expressed long ago in the divine command to love one's neighbor as oneself. But how are men to be changed so that they will have both the desire and the power so to act?

The idea of the "parliament of man" is no doubt derived from the House of Justice proposed by Baha'u'-llah, which would have full authority after the death of his two Branches, Abbas Effendi and Mirza Muhammad Ali. It was of course to be composed of Baha'is, and chosen by Baha'is, to rule over a Baha'i State. It would, therefore, be some time before this principle could be realized in practice. Meanwhile, the United Nations, composed mostly of "unbelievers," is trying to assist the people of the world to at least talk to each other.

Baha'u'llah commanded that Baha'is educate their children, and many of them have done this faithfully. The thought of "universal education" was introduced by Abdu'l-Baha after seeing what was done in this field in the West. And, finally, the command that "one language be chosen and taught to everybody" so that people would not disagree, was from Baha'u'llah, but it was never determined which language was to be used. Esperanto was tried for a time, but this effort was a failure.

Regarding Baha'i organization, the most important of Abdu'l-Baha's writings is his Last Will and Testament, a lengthy document in Persian and Arabic, which was published in 1924 in Cairo by the Baha'i Spiritual Assembly. It appears that the different portions of the Will were written at different times, some being quite early. The Will, in addition to other matters, contains (a) allegations against Subh-i-Azal, (b) allegations against Mirza Muhammad Ali, (c) allegations against

Mirza Badi'u'llah, (d) provisions for the Guardianship, and (e) provisions for the national and international Houses of Justice. Excerpts from the Will have been translated and published in English.

The portions of this document which are of principal interest to us are those which make provision for the leadership of the Baha'i Cause after the death of the Center of the Covenant. Baha'u'llah had made it quite clear in the *Kitab-i-Aqdas* and in his Will that on the death of his eldest son Abbas Effendi, the leadership was to go to a younger son, Mirza Muhammad Ali. He did not appoint a successor to Muhammad Ali, but commanded that thereafter matters should be referred to the House of Justice. One would have assumed that the man who called Himself the "Slave of Baha" would have scrupulously obeyed his father's command, but he appointed as his successor not his brother but his grandson Shoghi Effendi, with the title "Guardian of the Cause." We will quote some of the provisions of the Will as translated in the *Baha'i World*:

> O my loving friends! After the passing away of this wronged one, it is incumbent upon all believers to turn unto Shoghi Effendi . . . the guardian of the Cause of God. . . . He is the expounder of the words of God, and after him will succeed the first-born of his lineal descendants.
>
> It is incumbent upon the members of the House of Justice and upon all believers to show their obedience and subordination unto the guardian of the Cause of God, to turn unto him and be lowly before him.
>
> It is incumbent upon the guardian of the Cause of God to appoint in his own lifetime him that shall become his successor, that differences may not arise after his passing. He that is appointed must manifest in himself detachment from all worldly things, must be the essence of purity, must show in himself the fear of God, knowledge, wisdom and learning.

Thus, should the first-born of the guardian of the
Cause of God not manifest in himself the truth . . .
and his glorious lineage not be matched with a
goodly character, then must he [the guardian]
choose another branch to succeed him.

The Hands of the Cause of God must elect from
their own number nine persons that shall at all
times be occupied in the important services in the
work of the guardian of the Cause of God . . . and
these . . . must give their assent to the choice of
the one whom the guardian of the Cause of God
hath chosen as his successor.

And now concerning the House of Justice which
God hath ordained as the source of all good and
freed from all error, it must be elected by universal
suffrage, that is, by the believers. Its members
must be manifestations of the fear of God. . . . By
this House is meant the Universal House of Justice;
that is, in all countries a secondary House of Justice
must be instituted, and these secondary Houses of
Justice must elect the members of the Universal
one. Unto this body all things must be referred. . . .
Unto the Most Holy Book [*Kitab-i-Aqdas*] every
one must turn and all that is not expressly recorded
therein must be referred to the Universal House of
Justice. That which this body, whether unanimously
or by a majority doth carry, that is verily the Truth
and the Purpose of God Himself.

In closing his Will Abdu'l-Baha appeals again to all
Baha'is to be loyal to the Guardian. He writes:

O ye faithful loved ones of Abdu'l-Baha! It is incumbent upon you to take the greatest care of
Shoghi Effendi. . . . For he is, after Abdu'l-Baha,
the Guardian of the Cause of God. . . . He that
obeyeth him not hath not obeyed God; he that turneth away from him hath turned away from God. . . .
To none is given the right to put forth his own
opinion or express his particular convictions. All
must seek guidance and turn to the Center of the

Cause and the House of Justice. And he that turneth
unto whatsoever else is indeed in grievous error.

From these provisions for the future of the Cause it
is evident that, as Abdu'l-Baha, without ever calling himself a Manifestation, had assumed for himself the same
authority that had been claimed by Baha'u'llah, so by
bestowing absolute authority on Shoghi Effendi as the
infallible Guardian of the Cause of God, and by author-
izing Shoghi Effendi to appoint his son or one of his
lineal descendants as his successor, he intended to extend
indefinitely the Baha Manifestation, making it hereditary in his family. He commanded that the members of
the Universal House of Justice and the Hands of the
Cause and all believers must be completely obedient and
subservient to the Guardian, and no one was to question
anything he said or did. It is not clear how the command
for all believers to turn to the Most Holy Book (Kitab-i-
Aqdas) could have been obeyed, since no authorized
translation of this rare Arabic book had been published.

As for the establishment of Houses of Justice, in his
provisions in the Aqdas for these, Baha'u'llah anticipated
the time when some nation or nations would accept his
religion and would be ruled by a Baha'i government and
Baha'i laws. It seems that Abdu'l-Baha's plan for the
House of Justice was similar to his father's, for in his
Will he states:

> The House of Justice is the legislative authority and
> the government the executive power. The legisla-
> tive body must reinforce the executive; and the
> executive must aid and assist the legislative body,
> so that, through the connection and consolidation
> of these two forces, the foundation of fairness and
> justice may become firm and strong, that regions
> [of earth] may become . . . Paradise.

Thus, though Abdu'l-Baha knew that no nation would

adopt the Baha'i faith as its established religion in the near future, he nevertheless commanded that national Houses of Justice and an international House of Justice be established, and that Shoghi Effendi, as Guardian of the Cause of God, be the head of the Universal House of Justice. It is evident that so long as there was no government to enforce the decisions of the House of Justice, this body would function more like a church court than a political parliament, and many of the laws of the *Kitab-i-Aqdas* would be ineffectual. In the following chapter we will see how the commands of the Center of the Covenant were carried out by his grandson.

11

The Guardianship of Shoghi Effendi

THE DEATH OF ABDU'L-BAHA in 1921 marked the end of an era of Baha'i history, and the beginning of a new and different day. As Shoghi Effendi, the Guardian of the Cause of God, writes: "The Heroic, the Apostolic Age of the Dispensation of Baha'u'llah . . . had now terminated. . . . The Formative Period, the Iron Age, of that Dispensation was now beginning. . . ." The story of this "formative period," which is no doubt of importance to devoted Baha'is who are concerned about the development and growth of their Faith, is of much less general interest than the stirring events of the "heroic age." Baha'u'llah and his son Abdu'l-Baha were strong and impressive personalities. Whatever one may think of their claims and their conduct, they undoubtedly possessed great personal magnetism, and were able to win and hold the complete allegiance of numbers of people in the West as well as in the East. They also made many enemies who bitterly opposed them. In the new age there were no leaders of equal stature, and both the devotion and the animosity shown to the successor of Abdu'l-Baha were proportionately less.

In designating his grandson Shoghi as his successor, Abdu'l-Baha says of him in his Will:

> Behold, he is the blest and sacred bough that hath branched from the Twin Holy Trees . . . the most wondrous, unique and priceless pearl that doth gleam from out the twin surging seas. . . . He is the sign of God, the chosen branch, the guardian of the Cause of God. . . . He is the expounder of the words of God, and after him will succeed the first-born of his lineal descendants. . . . Whoso opposeth him hath opposed God.

The phrase "Twin Holy Trees" refers to Shoghi's parents. His mother was Ziyaiyya Khanum, eldest daughter of Abdu'l-Baha. His father was Mirza Hadi Afnan of Shiraz, a distant relative of the Bab. Shoghi was, therefore, a "branch" from the two holy families. He was born in Akka on March 3, 1896, and was designated as successor by Abdu'l-Baha when he was about ten years of age. His mother tongue was Persian, and he and his family knew Arabic, the language of the people of Akka and Haifa. He received an English and Arabic education at the American University of Beirut, but was not an outstanding student. One of his professors told the author that Shoghi was more interested in novels than in his studies. Later he was sent to Oxford University in England, and remained there till his grandfather died, when he returned to Haifa to assume the responsibilities of the Guardianship.

In March, 1923, the author was passing through Beirut on his way from Iran to America, and obtained a note of introduction to Shoghi Effendi from one of his former teachers. Having met a number of Baha'is during my residence in Iran, I was eager to see the new leader of the movement, and arranged to stop in Haifa on my way to Jerusalem. On my arrival I walked to his residence, presented the note of introduction, and received a warm welcome. Shoghi Effendi himself led me into his handsome and well-furnished home. He was a young man, short of stature and unimpressive in appearance, but courteous and friendly.

My host was most humble, making no claims for himself, and insisting that he was entirely unworthy of the great responsibility which had been laid upon him. When I requested that he kindly give me a picture of himself, he replied that he would prefer to give me one of his grandfather. This he did, writing on it an inscription in both Persian and English, the latter reading: "A Precious souvenir presented to my dear friend Mr. Miller, Haifa, Palestine, March 23, 1923. Shoghi Rabbani."

In answer to my questions Shoghi Effendi said that Baha'u'llah was not an Incarnation, for God is (in His Essence) beyond all reach, and cannot dwell in flesh and blood. He was rather a Manifestation of God, and in him all the attributes of God were found and could be known. The Bab who prepared the way for him, and Abdu'l-Baha who carried on his work after him, were quite different in rank from the Manifestation, for they were only divinely prepared men. Shoghi Effendi said that Abdu'l-Baha had not considered himself sinless, but used constantly to confess his sins and ask God for pardon. His grandfather had appointed Shoghi Effendi "to carry on the Movement," and he was busy organizing the World Council which was to be associated with him in this task. He stated that his principal effort would be to unite the "friends" of the East with those of the West.

When asked what the Baha'i religion had to offer which Christianity did not have, Shoghi Effendi replied that the principles of both were the same, and that only the outward forms differed; Baha'is simply believed that the teachings of Baha'u'llah were best for today (he did not specify why, or in what respects). He said that many people wanted to limit the Baha'i Cause, and narrow it, but it must be broad and include *all* religions, even Buddhism and other faiths, for all were from God. It was evident that the Guardian was more interested in the

organization and the ethical teachings of the Cause than
in its philosophical and theological foundations. Since
it was necessary for me to go on to Jerusalem, I was
unable to accept his gracious invitation to accompany
him to the shrine of Baha'u'llah in Akka.

In the earlier chapters of this book we have seen how,
after the deaths of the Bab and Baha'u'llah, bitter quarrels regarding the succession arose among the believers.
Fortunately, on the death of Abdu'l-Baha no one disputed the succession. This, however, did not indicate that
all the followers of Baha'u'llah welcomed the accession
of the Guardian, and were ready to obey him. We recall
that in the early years of the rule of Abdu'l-Baha, most
of the members of the family of Baha'u'llah vigorously
protested against what they considered to be unlawful
assumption of authority on the part of one who called
himself the "Slave of Baha," and as a result were rejected by Abdu'l-Baha. At the time of his death, the only
members of Baha'u'llah's family whom Abdu'l-Baha had
not rejected were his sister, his wife, his four daughters,
and their husbands. He showed great bitterness towards
his brothers Mirza Muhammad Ali and Mirza Badi'u'-
llah, and devoted large sections of his Will to denouncing
Mirza Muhammad Ali, charging his own followers to
avoid him altogether. Naturally, Mirza Muhammad Ali
and the members of the family who sympathized with
him were not ready to yield unquestioning obedience to
Abdu'l-Baha's grandson, especially since Baha'u'llah in
his Will ("My Covenant") had made it clear that after
his eldest son Abbas Effendi, the leader of the Baha'i
Cause was to be his second son Mirza Muhammad Ali.

During the life of Abdu'l-Baha, his brother Mirza
Muhammad Ali did not advance any claim to the leadership of the movement, though he did protest the pronouncements and acts of Abdu'l-Baha on the grounds
that they resembled those of a new Manifestation. When
Abdu'l-Baha died, why did not Mirza Muhammad Ali,

knowing that his father had specifically named him the successor to his brother, put forward his claim and declare himself the leader of the Cause and the infallible interpreter of the words of God? Why did he not dispute the appointment of Shoghi Effendi as Guardian as contrary to the *Kitab-i-Aqdas* and the Covenant of Baha'u'llah? The reason was twofold.

In the first place, Mirza Muhammad Ali was unwilling to refer the matter to a Muslim Court, where the Will and other writings of Baha would most certainly be investigated, and where his claim to be a Divine Manifestation and the founder of a new religion superior to Islam, which he and his followers had carefully concealed all the years they were in Akka, would be brought to light. This would be dangerous for all members of the family. For the same reason Shoghi Effendi never had his grandfather's Will probated in a court.

The second reason why Mirza Muhammad Ali did not press his claims was that Abdu'l-Baha had been successful in winning to his side the great majority of Baha'is, both in Iran and in the West, and had convinced them that Mirza Muhammad Ali was indeed¹ a wicked Covenant-breaker and an enemy of God. Mirza Muhammad Ali, therefore, knew in advance that any effort on his part to claim the heritage and position assigned to him by his father was sure to be rejected by those who revered Abdu'l-Baha as the Center of the Covenant and the infallible Expounder of the Baha'i teaching. Had Abdu'l-Baha not decreed that the successor should be Shoghi Effendi, the first Guardian of the Cause of God, and that he in turn should be succeeded by his eldest son? Whatever he decreed was the decree of God, and must be accepted. So Shoghi Effendi assumed the Guardianship unopposed.

When Shoghi Effendi realized the extent of the authority vested in him by the Will of Abdu'l-Baha, he proceeded to exercise his power. He demanded implicit obedience from the servants of God, in default of which they were liable to excommunication or summary expulsion from the faith. It is not surprising that this policy brought the Guardian into conflict not only with numerous believers but with the members of his own family, and resulted in their excommunication. The first to be purged was his grandmother, wife of Abdu'l-Baha and the first lady of the Baha'i realm. Eventually, all the members of Abdu'l-Baha's family, his daughters, his descendants, his sons-in-law, the brothers and sisters of Shoghi Effendi, and last of all Shoghi Effendi's own parents were excommunicated. Long-lasting family quarrels naturally resulted. Some of these had to do with the property which members of the family owned or occupied, and the fact that Abdu'l-Baba's Will had not been probated prevented any solution in the courts.

No doubt the Guardian was happy to turn away as much as possible from these family problems and direct his attention and energies to establishing the Administrative Order in which he was especially interested. He wrote to Baha'is in America and elsewhere instructing them to form, in every place where there were nine or more believers, Baha'i groups which would be called "Spiritual Assemblies." This was done, and in the *Baha'i World 1926-1928* the addresses of eighty-five Assemblies, most of them in America, are given. It was the function of these Assemblies to advance the Baha'i Cause in every way possible.

The next step was to form, in countries where the local groups had sufficiently advanced in numbers and influence, "National Assemblies," which had been designated in the Will of Abdu'l-Baha as "Secondary Houses of Justice," whose members were to be elected by the local Assemblies. The National Assemblies, in turn, were to elect the members of the "Universal House of Justice" provided for in the Will. In the *Baha'i World 1926-1928* nine National Assemblies are listed. The National Assemblies appointed National Committees responsible for the numerous aspects of the Cause's program, and a list of sixty-one committees has been supplied by Shoghi Effendi. How quickly the Cause of God became Americanized!

In 1926 the American Baha'i community adopted a National Constitution, which became the model for the other National Assemblies. A "Trust" was adopted and legally incorporated under the name, "The National Spiritual Assembly of the United States and Canada." Bylaws were also adopted, with regulations for membership, officers, and elections; these were later translated into other languages and used by Baha'is in other countries. After this incorporation of both National and Local Assemblies, it became possible for the Baha'i Cause to hold property and to receive gifts and endowments.

The Baha'i Cause having acquired a legal status, it became necessary to define membership. Who is a Baha'i? In one of his addresses in the United States Abdu'l-Baha was quoted as saying that "when Christians act in accordance with the teachings of Christ, they are called Baha'is." Clearly this definition would be inadequate for determining who might vote and hold office in the new organization. Concerning this important matter Shoghi Effendi wrote in 1925:

> Regarding the qualifications of a true believer . . . I would only venture to state very briefly . . . the principal factors: Full recognition of the station of the Forerunner [Bab], the Author [Baha'u'llah], and the True Exemplar of the Baha'i Cause as set forth in Abdu'l-Baha's *Testament* [Will]; unreserved acceptance of, and submission to whatsoever has been revealed by their Pen; loyal and steadfast adherence to every clause of our Beloved's sacred *Will;* and close association with the spirit as well as the form of the present-day Baha'i Administration throughout the world.

It might have been helpful to the American Baha'is who did not know Arabic and Persian if the Guardian had explained how they could make these promises when most of the writings of the Bab have been lost, and those that remain are not accessible, and even the Arabic *Kitab-i-Aqdas* of Baha'u'llah, to which so much importance was attached, had not at that time been translated into other languages and published by Baha'is. Undeterred by this question, 2584 persons declared themselves to be Baha'is in the United States Census of 1936.

While busy with affairs in other lands, the Guardian was also interested in establishing adequate facilities for the Cause in Haifa. Near the Mausoleum of the Bab and Abdu'l-Baha two "International Archives" were provided in which "priceless treasures" were deposited and displayed to visiting pilgrims.

> These included portraits of both the Bab and Baha'u'llah; personal relics such as the hair, the dust and garments of the Bab; the locks and blood of Baha'u'llah . . . His watch and His Qur'an; manuscripts and tablets of inestimable value . . . the *Persian Bayan*. . . .

There on Mt. Carmel, said Shoghi Effendi, "that permanent world Administrative Center of the future Baha'i Commonwealth" would eventually be established.

In *Baha'i News* of July, 1935, the Guardian wrote:

> Concerning membership in non-Baha'i religious associations, the Guardian wishes to re-emphasize the general principle already laid down . . . that no Baha'i who wishes to be a whole-hearted, sincere upholder of the distinguishing principles of the Cause can accept full membership in any non-Baha'i ecclesiastical organization.

This command undoubtedly disturbed believers in Muslim lands where such open profession would result in persecution, and also surprised some friends in the West who thought they could adopt Baha'i principles while maintaining membership in their churches. However, according to Shoghi Effendi, the loyal believers in East and West responded "through the severance of all ties of affiliation with, and membership in, ecclesiastical institutions of whatever denomination. . . . [Believers] have arisen to proclaim with one voice the independent character of the religion of Baha'u'llah."

Another problem which Shoghi Effendi had to face was internal dissension and the defection of some influential members of the Baha'i Cause, especially in the United States and in Iran. Many American members came to be closely identified with Mirza Ahmad Sohrab, born into a Baha'i family in Isfahan, Iran, and an intimate of Abdu'l-Baha and his close companion on the American tour in 1912. In 1919 Mirza Ahmad Sohrab came to the United States again, remaining there as a missionary. In New York he met Mrs. Lewis Chanler, an enthusiastic Baha'i. He remained there and lectured at the Baha'i Center. A group of those who heard him, led by Mrs. Chanler, founded "The New History Society" to further the Baha'i Cause. This incurred the wrath of the local Baha'i Administration which Shoghi Effendi supported. Their complaints eventually caused Shoghi Effendi to excommunicate both Ahmad Sohrab and Mrs. Chanler. Nevertheless, the New History Society expanded its work and opened the "Bahai Bookshop" in New York in 1939. The Spiritual Assembly claimed that this was illegal and brought suit, but in 1941 the Supreme Court of New York decided against them on the grounds that "the plaintiffs have no right to a monopoly of the name of a religion." Shoghi Effendi bitterly denounced his old friend Ahmad Sohrab. The latter detailed the whole controversy in a book, *Broken Silence*, maintaining that he was a true Baha'i. Ahmad Sohrab accepted Shoghi Effendi as Guardian but insisted that he was despotic in the use of his authority. Actually, the controversy was a power struggle between two ambitious men. It is not known how many devoted believers, like Mrs. Chanler, were lost to the Cause through this conflict.

While Sohrab, Mrs. Chanler, and their companions in America went their own way, devoted to the Baha'i Cause, there were several of its former leaders in Iran who not only repudiated the Administration, but wrote and published books, telling in detail why they had defected. One of these defectors was a man named H. Niku, who had been a Baha'i for fourteen years, and one of the leading missionaries of the Cause. In Persian publications entitled *The Philosophy of Niku*, he described the disillusioning things which he had seen and heard — the worldly ambition of Abdu'l-Baha, his greed for money, and his flattering epistles to great and wealthy people whom he hoped to win as disciples.

Another man who deserted the Cause was Ayati, to whom Abdu'l-Baha had given the name Avareh (Wanderer). For twenty-one years Avareh was a Baha'i; he was appointed one of the Hands of the Cause, became one of the movement's outstanding writers and missionaries, and was greatly revered by the Baha'is. Abdu'l-Baha commissioned him to write the official history of the Babi-Baha'i movement, which he did in Persian.

Avareh served Shoghi Effendi for a number of years, and was sent to Europe to make converts, but on his return he left the Movement. After coming back to Iran he was excommunicated by the Guardian. He then wrote a three-volume book in Persian entitled *Kashfu'l-Hiyal* (The Exposure of Deception), in which he related how he had become a Baha'i, and why he had defected. He said that before he left Iran he had been told that there were millions of Baha'is in Europe and America, and he had believed it. Later when he went to Akka he began to discover the fraud and corruption which existed at the center of the Cause, and his faith began to waver. He said that when he wrote the history of the Movement,

Abdu'l-Baha forced him to misrepresent the facts, insisting that there should be no discrepancy between the new history and *A Traveller's Narrative* (written by Abdu'l-Baha).

A third Iranian Baha'i leader to desert the Cause was Mirza Subhi, member of a Baha'i family, and a relative of the third wife of Baha'u'llah. For a number of years he was the Persian amanuensis of Abdu'l-Baha, and was intimately acquainted with all members of his family, including Shoghi Effendi before he became Guardian. Later, he was sent to Iran for missionary work, but there he began to show a lack of zeal in the service of the Cause, and was excommunicated by Shoghi Effendi. As a result, Subhi was unable to find employment in Teheran, for Muslims rejected him as a Baha'i agent, and Baha'is rejected him as an apostate from their faith. It was then that a friend found him a position in a Christian mission school, saving him from dire need. He later became a famous teller of stories to children on Teheran radio. Subhi wrote two books in Persian explaining why he had given up the Baha'i religion.

Like his grandfather and great-grandfather, Shoghi Effendi was a prolific writer. He wrote reams of letters to the believers in America and other lands. These letters have been published in several volumes entitled *Messages to America, Messages to the Baha'i World, Baha'i Administration,* and so on. Shoghi Effendi rendered an important literary service to the Baha'i Cause by translating several Baha'i books into English. For some reason he did not translate the *Kitab-i-Aqdas,* which he called "the Mother-Book of the Baha'i Revelation," nor did he undertake the codification of the laws and ordinances contained in this basic document of Baha'i faith and government. Perhaps the most pretentious work from the pen of the Guardian was *God Passes By,* a book of more than four hundred pages, which purports to be a history of the Babi-Baha'i Movement during the first

century of its existence (1844-1944). This volume is a
mine of information, not all of which, unfortunately, is
accurate. It is the fourth official Baha'i history, the first
three being the *New History* and *A Traveller's Narrative* by Abdu'l-Baha, and *Nabil's Narrative*, an account
of the early days of the Movement which was translated
and published by Shoghi Effendi under the title *The
Dawn Breakers*. Nabil was one of those Babis who
claimed to be He-Whom-God-Will-Manifest during the
Baghdad period, but he later withdrew his claim and
became a disciple of Baha'u'llah. In his history, Shoghi
Effendi failed to give any documentary support whatever for his statements, perhaps on the assumption that
statements of the infallible expositor of the Words of
God needed no such confirmation. The book would be
far more valuable had the author made use of the early
Nuqtatu'l-Kaf of Mirza Jani, and depended less on the
late and inaccurate accounts of Nabil and Abdu'l-Baha.

Regarding the historical value of these various accounts, one who knows the history well has written:

> By the passage of time Baha'i accounts have assumed
> a chameleonic character, totally divorced from truth.
> Simple events and incidents are distorted and mis-
> represented in the furtherance of private ends and
> personal ambitions. The cases treated in these pages
> [*God Passes By*] are glaring examples of misrepre-
> sentations of historical facts.

It was said that when Shoghi Effendi was a student in
Beirut he was very fond of reading novels, and *God
Passes By* should be considered an historical novel
rather than authentic history.

In reading this book one is disappointed to find that
the Guardian of a Cause which has professed allegiance
to peace, love, world-brotherhood, and the absence of any
sort of prejudice, should have expressed such bitterness
toward many members of his own family. He refers to
Baha'u'llah's second son Mirza Muhammad Ali as "the

Prime Mover of sedition"; he speaks of the third and
fourth sons as "The vacillating Mirza Diya'u'llah and the
treacherous Mirza Badi'u'llah"; and he calls the sons-in-
law of Baha'u'llah "infamous" and "crafty." In his Messages also the Guardian sometimes condemned with great
severity those who differed with him. In a cablegram
addressed to the Baha'is of the United States, he announced the death of Sayyid Ali, a grandson of Baha'u'-
llah and husband of Shoghi's eldest sister. It is said that
Sayyid Ali "had a charming personality, and associated
with, and befriended, men of all walks of life." But he
strongly expressed his opposition to the Guardian's policy
of rejecting anyone who did not fully agree with him,
and as a result he was excommunicated. The three hun-
dred-word cable begins thus:

> God's Avenging Wrath
>   Inform National Assemblies [that] God's aveng-
> ing wrath . . . [has] now struck down . . . Siyyid
> Ali Nayer Afnan, pivot [of] Machinations, connect-
> ing link [between] old [and] new Covenant-break-
> ers. This alone [will] reveal extent [of] havoc
> wreaked [by] this virus [of] violation injected,
> fostered over two decades [in] Abdul Baha's family.
> . . . [who] was repeatedly denounced by Center
> [of the] Covenant [as] his chief enemy. . . .

Thus did the Guardian announce to the friends in
America the decease of his brother-in-law. He was, of
course, only following the example of Baha'u'llah who
so denounced his brother Subh-i-Azal, and of Abdu'l-
Baha's recriminatory charges against his brother Mirza
Muhammad Ali in his Will. If these characterizations of
members of the family of Baha'u'llah were true, it would
seem that the Manifestation was not particularly successful in training his own children. If the characterizations
were false, they do not speak well for the infallibility
of the Guardian.

The key figure in the development of the Baha'i Move-

ment in America during the Guardianship of Shoghi
Effendi was Horace Holley, whose executive and literary
efforts were outstanding. It was he who drafted the official Administrative Order of the National Spiritual
Assembly of America, which became the model for other
Assemblies around the world; it was he who edited the
large volume entitled *Baha'i Scriptures*. As Secretary of
the National Spiritual Assembly from 1924 to 1955 he
edited the Cause's large and informative yearbook, *Baha'i
World*, and wrote a number of the leading articles in
each volume. Over a period of thirty years, Holley published twelve volumes of the *Baha'i World;* the edition
for 1940-1944 alone comprises 1003 pages. These volumes
contain detailed information concerning the progress of
the Baha'i Cause throughout the world, many pictures
of groups of converts in various countries, reprints of
the Baha'i Constitution and By-Laws in a number of
languages, commendations of the Cause from the pens
of numerous notables, lists of places where there are
Assemblies or Groups of believers, and lists of books and
periodicals favorable to the Cause (critical accounts are
not usually listed). Holley also wrote several books about
the Faith. He died on July 12, 1960.

One of the great achievements which brought joy to
many Baha'i hearts was the completion of the Mashriqu'l-
Adhkar in Wilmette, Illinois. As related in Chapter 9,
the ground for this Temple was dedicated by Abdu'l-
Baha in 1912, but the plans were large and the friends
were few, so the task was tremendous. Plans for a unique
and beautiful structure were drawn and construction
began in 1920. In 1925 a three-year drive to collect
$400,000 for this building was undertaken by the National
Spiritual Assembly. The superstructure was completed in
1931, and a devotional service was conducted in the Temple just nineteen years after the dedication of the land.
The beautification of the structure continued for twelve

more years, and was completed in December, 1942, shortly before the Centenary in 1944. It had taken twenty-two
and a half years to build the Temple, the first to be
erected in the West, and the total cost was $1,342,813.

In preparation for the observance of the 1944 Centenary of the Movement, a "Seven Year Plan" in true
American style was adopted in 1937 by the National
Spiritual Assembly. Its aim was to make new converts
to the Cause, and to establish a Spiritual Assembly in
every state and province in North America which did not
yet have one. Accordingly, there was a burst of missionary zeal in the ranks of the believers, and in seven years
the number of Assemblies in North America rose from
seventy to 124, with thirty-four new areas being opened.
Since it was the policy of the Administration not to
report the number of members, it is not known how many
new converts were made during this period.

An aggressive campaign to extend the Faith was carried on under the guidance of the Guardian not only in
North America but in other lands as well. The order went
out from Haifa that Baha'is should become "pioneers,"
leave their homes, go to the unoccupied places, and establish Groups (less than nine members) which would grow
into Assemblies (more than nine members). Missionaries from North America went south and established
centers in a number of cities in South America, and they
went also to European countries and to other lands. It
seems that growth in Great Britain was slow. In writing
of the missionary service of these pioneers of the Faith,
Shoghi Effendi said that most of the activities

> have been carried out through the resourcefulness
> of the members of the American Baha'i Community,
> who have assumed direct responsibility for the spir-
> itual conquest of the vast majority of these coun-
> tries.

Missionaries also went forth to other lands from Iran.

It was reported that they opened a hundred new centers in East Africa.

In 1948 the political situation in Palestine changed radically, and Akka and Haifa became a part of Israel. Though the Baha'is had been closely linked to the Muslim Arabs in the past, it seems that the new Government accepted their presence and afforded them the same liberty which they had enjoyed under the British Mandate. The President visited the shrine of the Bab and called on Shoghi Effendi. Israel was no doubt the more ready to tolerate the presence of this non-Jewish institution in Haifa because of its value as a tourist attraction, and because the Baha'is there seem to have given up the Muslim customs which they followed prior to the death of Abdu'l-Baha, and also because no effort had been made to convert others in Israel to the Baha'i Faith. It is said that most of the Iranian Baha'is left Israel voluntarily, or were sent away by Shoghi Effendi.

During this period, how was the Baha'i Cause faring in Iran, the land of its birth? Because of the necessity for avoiding publicity, there is not a great deal to be found in the volumes of the *Baha'i World* regarding the progress of the Faith in Iran, where the majority of the Baha'is of the world resided. The first National Convention of Baha'is was held in Teheran in 1934, and about the same time the first National Spiritual Assembly in Iran was organized. In 1940 the large and impressive Haziratu'l-Quds (Headquarters) was completed in Teheran. Many believers and their friends frequently assembled there for various activities, but Baha'i activity often resulted in increased opposition from fanatical Muslims. In 1955, when anti-Baha'i feeling was strong in the country, the large dome of the Haziratu'l-Quds was destroyed, and the property was taken over by the government, although it was later restored to the Baha'is. It is impossible to estimate the number of Baha'is in Iran at this time. However, the period of persecution was short-lived, and soon the Baha'is carried on as usual in the bazaar and elsewhere. They are hated by confirmed Muslims because they hold that Baha'u'llah has taken the place of Muhammad, whom Muslims consider to be the last great prophet and the "Seal" of the Prophets. It is true that on the whole they are more progressive than many Muslims, and, since "honesty is the best policy," they may be more honest in business than members of some other religious groups.

It is surprising to turn the thousands of pages of the twelve large volumes of the *Baha'i World* from 1921 to 1954 and find no pictures of the Guardian of the Cause, and very little information about his life and his labors for the Faith. It seems that for some reason Shoghi Effendi did not desire this kind of publicity. His residence was always in Haifa, and he seldom visited other lands, never following the steps of his grandfather in making grand tours of Europe and America. Having excommunicated most of the members of his own family, his life must have been a somewhat lonely one.

Shoghi Effendi was to have married his cousin Maryam, daughter of Mirza Jalal Shahid, but decided not to do so. Finally, in 1937 when he was forty-one years of age, he married Mary Maxwell, to whom he gave the name Ruhiyyih Khanum (Lady Spiritual). East and West were united in this marriage. Mary, born in 1910, was the daughter of May Bolles, a Canadian who had been a member of the first party of Americans to visit Akka in 1898, and who from that time till her death devoted herself to the propagation of the Baha'i Faith. In 1923 mother and daughter spent seven months in Haifa; they visited the Guardian again in 1937 and assisted him in his work. It was then that Shoghi Effendi chose Mary to be his wife. Their marriage continued for twenty years, and Ruhiyyih Khanum acted as her husband's secretary for sixteen of them. They were not blessed with children.

Shoghi Effendi and his wife went to London in October, 1957, to order furniture and fixings for the Archives Building on Mt. Carmel in which both were deeply interested. Shoghi Effendi also went to seek medical advice, since his health was not good. On October 27 he felt quite unwell. His wife also became ill, and the physician who visited them said they both had Asiatic influenza and ordered rest. Ruhiyyih Khanum recovered after a few days, but Shoghi Effendi did not and on the morning of November 4, when Ruhiyyih Khanum went to his room, she found him dead. The doctor said he had suffered a heart attack, and had died peacefully in sleep. Friends and Hands of the Cause who were not in London hurried there to help the heart-broken widow. They were greatly concerned that the body of the Guardian be buried exactly in accordance with the laws laid down by Baha'u'llah in the *Kitab-i-Aqdas*. "God has commanded," wrote Baha'u'llah, "that the dead be buried in [coffins of] crystal or rare stones or beautiful hard woods, and that engraved rings be placed on their fingers. Indeed, He is the Knower, the Predeterminer."

The problem which greatly concerned Ruhiyyih Khanum and the other Hands was finding a suitable place of burial which, in obedience to the law of the *Aqdas*, would be not more than an hour's journey from London. After considerable search they discovered an ideal spot in the Great Northern Cemetery at New Southgate; a plot was purchased immediately, and four small cypress trees were planted at the four corners, "in memory of the hundreds of cypress trees that the beloved Guardian had planted . . . around the Holy Places in Bahji and Haifa." All was made ready for the burial in "a strong, deep vault."

The funeral took place on November 9. It was reported in full by the Baha'i Publishing Trust. A few lines are quoted here:

All stood while the wonderful prayer, ordained by

Baha'u'llah for the dead, was chanted in Arabic. Six other prayers and excerpts from the Teachings were then read by friends with beautiful voices, some in English, some in Persian, and representative Baha'is from Europe, Africa, America, Asia — Negro, Jew, and Aryan.

The casket was then taken to the grave, and

as all stood, silently waiting for the coffin to be lowered into the grave, Ruhiyyih Khanum asked that it be announced that before the coffin was placed in the grave, the friends who wished might pass by it and pay their respects. For over two hours the believers, eastern and western, filed by. For the most part they knelt and kissed the edge or the handle of the casket. Rarely indeed in history can such a demonstration of love and grief have been seen.

Shoghi Effendi, great-grandson of Baha'u'llah, had been gathered to his fathers, and buried far from his fathers' native land. Speedily, the Hands of the Cause of God made their way to Haifa to read the Will of the Guardian, and learn what provision he had made for a successor.

12

The Rule of the People

SEVERAL MONTHS BEFORE his execution in July, 1850, the Bab appointed Subh-i-Azal as his successor. Sixteen years after the death of the Bab, Baha'u'llah repudiated Subh-i-Azal's appointment, and declared that he himself was a new Manifestation. In his Will he appointed his two eldest sons to succeed him in turn, first Abbas Effendi, and after him Mirza Muhammad Ali. But Abbas, better known as Abdu'l-Baha, ignored his father's Will, and in his own Will appointed his grandson Shoghi Effendi as his successor and Guardian of the Cause of God, stipulating that he should be succeeded by his eldest son. But when Shoghi Effendi died in 1957, he left no Will and appointed no successor, thereby violating both the command of Baha'u'llah that "the writing of a Will has been made incumbent on everyone," and also the provision in the Will of Abdu'l-Baha that he should "appoint in his own lifetime him that shall become his successor, that differences may not arise after his passing." "After him will succeed the first-born of his lineal descendants." In case the first-born was not worthy, Shoghi Effendi was to "choose another branch to succeed him." Since the Guardian died childless, and no Branch therefore existed, he may be forgiven for his failure to carry out this provision in his grandfather's

Will, a document on which he had leaned heavily for his authority.

But why did not Shoghi Effendi write a Will? Had he not read the *Kitab-i-Aqdas,* which, he had said, "may well be regarded as the brightest emanation of the mind of Baha'u'llah, as the Mother Book of His Dispensation, and the Charter of His New World Order?" Had death overtaken him unprepared? Or was he, though infallible, unable to solve the problem of the succession, or unwilling to continue playing the game of Divinity? By failing to leave a Will, was he intentionally ending the Guardianship? Perhaps his wife and close friends knew what was in the mind of Shoghi Effendi, but if they knew they have not divulged his secret to others.

It seems clear that the Hands of the Cause, appointed by the Guardian to assist him in everything, were not expecting this eventuality. According to *Time* magazine, twenty-six of the twenty-seven Hands hastened to Haifa shortly after the death of the Guardian, and "ransacked the headquarters. . . . They searched Shoghi Effendi's safe box without success. All week long they met in secret session. . . ." At last they announced the solution: "there would be no new Guardian at all, but a nine-man council of Hands at Haifa, titled 'Hands of the Cause of God on Holy Land.' The new body [will] have no powers to interpret scripture." About three weeks after the death of Shoghi Effendi, the Hands issued a long statement, explaining to the Baha'is of the world what they had done. In this they said: "In our capacity as Chief Stewards of the embryonic World Commonwealth of Baha'u'llah, we Hands of the Cause have constituted a body of nine Hands to serve at the Baha'i World Centre." The document was signed by all twenty-six of the Hands who were in Haifa.

The Hands inherited a truly difficult problem. Since Shoghi Effendi had no offspring, he could not appoint a successor in accordance with Abdu'l-Baha's Will, and

Abdu'l-Baha had made no provision for the succession
in case Shoghi Effendi should be childless. Hence, as the
Hands realized, there was no way to appoint a successor
in conformity to the Will. Abdu'l-Baha was mistaken in
the supposition that there would be Guardians in his
family for generation after generation.

The plan which the Hands adopted was that the Universal House of Justice, in accordance with the provision
in the Will of Abdu'l-Baha, should at last be established,
and should head the Baha'i Faith. But had they forgotten
that the same Will stipulated that the head of the House
of Justice must be the Guardian, or someone appointed
by him? Therefore, without a Guardian or someone
appointed by him to preside over the Universal House of
Justice, this body, when elected, would have no head —
and headless bodies do not usually function helpfully.
Moreover, according to the Will, the Hands of the Cause
were to be appointed by the Guardian, were to turn
to him, and guard him, and "be occupied in the important services in the work of the Guardian." But if there
were no Guardian, whom would the Hands obey, and
whom would they serve? Hands without a head to direct
them are at best ineffective. Accordingly, if the Will of
Abdu'l-Baha is to be taken as authoritative, the whole
Baha'i structure — Guardianship, Hands of the Cause of
God, and Universal House of Justice — collapsed with the
death of Shoghi Effendi. It must have seemed to some
that God had failed them, or, as others explained the
situation, that He had changed His mind about the
future of His Cause.

What, then, could the devoted Hands who gathered
in Haifa do to rescue the Cause of God from extinction?
Apparently, they did the only thing possible under the
circumstances: they ignored the provisions of the Will
of Abdu'l-Baha regarding the Guardianship, but retained
the institutions of the Hands of the Cause and the National and Universal Assemblies prescribed by Him, and

went back to the provisions in the *Kitab-i-Aqdas* and the Will of Baha'u'llah, according to which the affairs of the Cause, after the deaths of the two Branches, Abbas Effendi and Mirza Muhammad Ali, were to be ordered by the House of Justice.

Were there no loyal believers in the infallibility of Abdu'l-Baha present at Haifa to protest this treatment of the Center of the Covenant, the Exponent of the Word of God? Only the Hands know what was said in the secret sessions, and they, having been sworn to secrecy, with one exception have revealed nothing. It is indeed amazing how easily the great majority of Baha'is seemed to forget immediately all that had been said and written about the absolute indispensability of the Guardianship, and accepted cheerfully and without question the more democratic rule of the Universal House of Justice.

There was, however, one Hand who had a better memory and greater reverence for the Will of the Master than the rest. He was Charles Mason Remey, a member of the Custodian Hands in Haifa. Mr. Remey, born in 1874, a member of an eminent American family, was reared as a Christian, and educated as an architect. He became a Baha'i in 1899 when he was a young man, and served the Cause zealously for many years. In 1909-1910 he made a round-the-world tour on behalf of his faith. He wrote many books and pamphlets about the Baha'i Cause. For many years his name appeared frequently in the Baha'i records. He was appointed to draw the plans for the Archives Building on Mt. Carmel and the Baha'i temples in Africa and Australia. Shoghi Effendi called Mason Remey to Haifa, where he remained for ten years, made him a Hand of the Cause, and, in 1951, when he established the first International Baha'i Council, which, according to Shoghi Effendi, would eventually become the Universal House of Justice, he appointed Remey its President. Shoghi Effendi always gave Mason Remey the place of honor next to himself. When Shoghi Effendi died the Government of Israel gave the name of Mason Remey as "the New Head of the Baha'i Faith" in their official yearbook for 1957.

Mr. Remey has stated in his various writings that, since both Abdu'l-Baha and the First Guardian had made it clear that there must always be a Guardian, after the death of Shoghi Effendi he earnestly tried to persuade the other Hands that the Guardianship must be continued, but they all refused to listen to him. Gradually he decided that since Shoghi Effendi had made him the President of the International Council, he himself was the successor appointed by the First Guardian. He says that he waited more than two years for the Hands in Haifa to realize this fact, and on their own initiative to concur in his assuming the leadership as the Second Guardian. However, it became evident that they did not want to have a Second Guardian, and were gradually preparing the believers to accept a new type of organization. So, at the end of 1959, he left the Hands in Haifa, returned to America, and in April, 1960, issued a statement proclaiming himself the Guardian, and calling on all Baha'is to accept him. His printed "Proclamation to the Baha'is of the World" was sent to the Annual Convention of Baha'is of the U.S.A. meeting in Wilmette, Illinois. After detailing his reasons for claiming the Guardianship and the grounds on which he based his claim, Remey said, "I am now declaring my position of command in the Cause to believers here in America . . . and through this Convention to all the Baha'i World." He then ordered the Hands in Haifa to desist at once from their plans to elect the Universal House of Justice, and said, "I alone in all the world have been given the authority and the power to accomplish this. . . . It is from and through the Guardianship that infallibility is vested and that the Hands of the Faith receive their orders." He said that he based his authority on his appointment by Shoghi Effendi to the Presidency of the International Council. It seems that this plea for fidelity to the Guardianship and to him as Second Guardian fell largely on deaf ears, for the Hands went ahead with their plans for 1963, and only a small minority of Baha'is rallied about the Second Guardian. The majority, perhaps wearied by the demands of a Divine dictator, had discovered that the Guardian had not been infallible, and desired to change to a more democratic form of government for the Cause.

In 1960 Mr. Remey published a small fifty-two-page book entitled *A Last Appeal to the Hands of the Faith,* in which, with a conciliatory spirit and at great length, he exhorted the Hands

> to abandon their program for 1963, that they seek to find the Second Guardian of the Baha'i Faith, and that they uphold the Will and Testament of the Master Abdu'l-Baha and the Administration of the Faith as established by the Beloved Guardian Shoghi Effendi.

In this *Last Appeal* Mr. Remey states that at one of the secret sessions of the Hands the ten Iranians proposed that, under the circumstances, the Guardianship of the Faith must be considered to be ended and that, "in the confusion and heat of the moment," this was voted by a majority of the conclave. He goes on to argue that without the institution of the Guardianship there can be no Administration — the two are one and co-existent. He continues:

> For the past year and more I've tried to use gentle and pacific reasons for arguments in defence of the Guardianship against the united intention of the body of the Hands that there shall never be another Guardian. Now seeing that this violation of the Master's Will and Testament is daily becoming stronger until it threatens to become the accepted way of life of the Cause, as a last resort I am

> obliged single handedly to come out into the open
> and use my prerogatives as President of the Inter-
> national Baha'i Council as appointed by our late
> Beloved Guardian, to force the Hands of the Faith
> to relinquish their united stand against the Guard-
> ianship. . . . My way of forcing this issue is simply
> by announcing to the Hands that in no way shall I
> countenance their right to do anything at all about
> or with the Baha'i International Council. . . . I take
> the stand that there can be no functioning of the
> Council until there be a recognized and accepted
> Guardian of the Faith to institute it. The Hands of
> the Faith have no right to command the election of
> an International Council. . . . In other words, I block
> their actions in this. . . .

Mason Remey says that he had kept his promise and
had discussed these secret matters only with the Hands
of the Faith. But after two years of earnest effort, having failed to convince the other Hands that they were
violating the Will and Testament, he felt that he was
forced to break with them, to announce that he as President of the International Council was the one appointed
by the First Guardian to succeed him, and that he therefore no longer felt bound by his promise to keep these
matters secret.

Did it ever occur to Mr. Remey that, in claiming to
be the Guardian, he was himself violating the Will,
which required that the successor to the Guardian be
"the first-born of his lineal descendants," or "another
branch," another of his children? And had he never
read the provision for the succession made in Baha'u'-
llah's Will, and realized that, in appointing Shoghi
Effendi as Guardian, Abdu'l-Baha had violated his
father's Will? It is probably too much to expect that
he should have delved deeply enough into the early
history of the Movement to discover that Baha'u'llah, in
claiming to be a Manifestation, had flagrantly violated
the Bab's provision for *his* successor. Had Mason Remey

known more of Baha'i history he would probably not have been so amazed at the conduct of the Hands of the Faith during this crisis.

In later statements and pamphlets, Mr. Remey, as self-proclaimed Second Guardian, predicted that a terrible catastrophe was impending, in which two-thirds of the population of the world would perish. In 1961 he removed all his personal records from Chicago to Santa Fe, New Mexico, seven thousand feet above sea level. He himself resided in Florence, Italy, on one of the hills higher than the inundations that were to occur. In 1967, when ninety-three years of age, he wrote to friends that Shoghi Effendi was mistaken in his teachings, and that, while Baha'u'llah was infallible, Abdu'l-Baha made mistakes in some of his statements.

In 1968 Mason Remey announced the appointment of "the first five Elders of the Baha'i Epoch," from four countries. Donald Harvey was the first Elder, and the probable appointee as Remey's successor. Remey also urged believers to pay the tax prescribed in the *Kitab-i-Aqdas,* to cover the expenses of the office in Florence. He chose for those loyal to him the name, "The Orthodox Abha World Faith." The minority of Baha'is loyal to the "Hereditary Guardianship" of Mason Remey carried on various activities in America and Pakistan and some other lands. For several years, from headquarters in Santa Fe, they published *The Glad Tidings — A Bulletin of the Baha'is Under the Hereditary Guardianship,* containing messages from the Second Guardian and news of the progress of the "true" Baha'i Faith. A National Spiritual Assembly was organized, and was registered by the U.S. Government as a separate organization from that of the Baha'is with headquarters at Wilmette, who rejected Remey. Lawsuits between the two factions ensued, and were finally decided in favor of the Wilmette party. It seems that Mason Remey was not involved in these suits; in fact he told his followers to desist, and to dissolve their

National Spiritual Assembly, which they did. However, he was disturbed by dissension among his followers, and wrote them a strong letter about the evil of backbiting and quarreling, and the danger of becoming so involved in problems of administration that they would reject their primary duty to give spiritual teaching to needy people.

Though Mason Remey loyally supported the Baha'i Administration's thirty-six-year-old tenet that it was God's will, and absolutely essential to the Cause, that there always be an Infallible Guardian, he was rejected by the great majority of the world's Baha'is, who made every effort to minimize the importance of the schism which had occurred in the Faith. The only reference to it in *The Baha'i World* is on page 353 of vol. XIII, where "yet another severe test" is mentioned. This veiled statement is explained by the following footnote:

> The defection of Mason Remey, who after signing the Proclamation of November 25, 1957, claimed in April, 1960, to be the "hereditary Guardian" of the Cause of God. This attempt to create schism in the Faith resulted in his expulsion by the Hands of the Cause.

Mason Remey died in his residence in Florence, Italy, on February 4, 1974, just ninety-nine days before his one hundredth birthday.

The decision to dispense with the Guardianship was as radical a step for the Baha'is to take as a vote by the Cardinals to abolish the Papacy would be for the Roman Catholics, yet that is what they did. It seems that there were many who had resented the dictatorship of Shoghi Effendi, but had submitted to his absolute control of the Movement out of necessity. The death of the Guardian gave them an opportunity to free themselves, and they promptly did so. Hence, for the first time in more than a century the majority of the members of the Movement found themselves without a living head whom they held to be divinely appointed and infallible.

However important the Universal House of Justice may seem to be in the eyes of the Baha'is, it is quite evident that the real rulers of the Cause of God after the death of Shoghi Effendi were the nobles of the realm, the Hands of the Cause, of whom the most influential was probably Ruhiyyih Khanum, the widow of the Guardian, one of the two Living Hands who were women. Since the Hands were aging and some had died, and no others were to be appointed in their place, they chose numerous members of "Auxiliary Boards" in different lands to assist them in propagating the Faith; the Universal House of Justice, in consultation with the Hands, established a dozen "Continental Boards of Counsellors" for the same purpose. Ruhiyyih Khanum and three other Hands resided in Haifa; other Hands were assigned to twelve different parts of the world in which the Continental Boards had been established.

From past experience the leaders of the Cause knew well the value of frequent conferences and assemblies to celebrate the important events in the history of the movement, both to increase the zeal of the believers and to impress the outside world. Hence, following close on the 1963 Congress in London, more great meetings were planned for 1967. These were to celebrate "the centenary of Baha'u'llah's proclamation of his Message in 1867 to the kings and rulers of the world. . . ," and also to celebrate the hundred-fiftieth anniversary of his birth.

The Baha'i News of December, 1967, contains reports of the six Intercontinental Conferences held simultaneously in Panama City, Wilmette, Sydney, Kampala, Frankfurt, and New Delhi. In Panama, Ruhiyyih Khanum laid the cornerstone of the temple to be erected there and addressed the assembly. At Wilmette, where three thousand Baha'is gathered, three Hands of the Cause, the oldest of whom was Mr. Samandari of Iran, who had seen Baha'u'llah with his own eyes, made addresses, and there was a telephone hook-up with the five other Conferences. When an appeal was made for pioneers to serve the Cause, 216 persons came forward as volunteers.

The Conferences in Frankfurt, Kampala, New Delhi, and Sydney were not as large as that in Wilmette, but they were no less enthusiastic in their welcome to the Hands who visited them and in their devotion to the memory of Baha'u'llah. It seems that by this time all had become used to the idea that the Universal House of Justice, which claimed infallibility for itself, had taken the place of the infallible Guardian, and no explanation or defense of this transfer of authority is found in the reports of the Conferences. A new day had dawned in the history of the Cause.

In 1964 the Universal House of Justice adopted a "Nine Year Plan" for achieving certain goals by 1973; one of those goals was to improve greatly the property of the World Center on Mt. Carmel at Haifa. Large budgets were adopted to make this possible; the 1967-1968 budget in the U.S.A. being $1,060,000, of which twenty-one per cent was to go to the World Center. More than half of the budget was to come from endowments and publications, and the balance (about $450,000) was to be supplied by contributions from the seventeen thousand Baha'is in the U.S.A., an average gift of twenty-seven dollars from each member for the year.

However, the chief goal of the Nine Year Plan was to get new members. To this end aggressive efforts were made to inform and interest people in the Cause, and to convert them to it. At the Convention in Wilmette in 1967 it was reported that in Canada there was a "plan for six annual phases of proclamation, each directed towards a particular segment of the population."

In the U.S.A. the campaign for new members was headed by a retired Air Force officer who was chairman of the National Teaching Committee. It was reported that he was assisted by nine hundred public information representatives located throughout the country. Proclamation of the Baha'i Cause concentrated on major media promotion and public meetings for seven special events: World Peace Day (September 15), United Nations Day (October 24), Birthday of Baha'u'llah (November 12), Human Rights Day (December 10), World Religion Day (January 19), No Ruz (the Iranian New Year, March 21), and Race Unity Day (June 8). By taking an active part in these events Baha'is hoped that they would make numerous contacts with interested people, who could then be brought into "firesides," that is, meetings in private homes. Films were also shown describing "the progress of the Baha'i Faith in over 56,000 localities throughout the world."

Those who are persuaded to become members of the Baha'i Faith "declare" themselves to be Baha'is by signing a card which is then forwarded to Wilmette. The card reads as follows: "I _____ [signature] accept the qualifications of the faith as defined on reverse side of this card, and apply for enrollment as member of the Baha'i community." On the reverse side is the statement by Shoghi Effendi:

> The principal factors that must be taken into consideration before deciding whether a person may be regarded as a true believer or not . . . [are] Full recognition of the station of the Forerunner [the Bab], the Author [Baha'u'llah], and the True Exemplar [Abdu'l-Baha] of the Baha'i Cause, as set forth in Abdu'l-Baha's Testament; unreserved acceptance of, and submission to, whatsoever has been revealed by their Pen; loyal and steadfast adherence to every clause of our Beloved's sacred Will; and close association with the spirit as well as the form of the present day Baha'i administration throughout the world.

It would seem that for one to sign this statement with

understanding and honesty he would have to spend many
months in study; one would need to know both the Persian and Arabic languages to be able to read the considerable volume of extant and available writings "revealed by their Pen." And if the applicant for membership were able to do all this, which probably no living
Baha'i has done, could he today give "steadfast adher-
ence" to the clauses of Abdu'l-Baha's Will requiring
that there always be a Guardian in the line of Shoghi
Effendi, when the Cause is now without a Guardian? It
seems, however, that these considerations have not de-
terred eager applicants from becoming devoted converts
to the Cause. When the card, signed by the new believer,
has been sent to headquarters, the convert is entitled to
attend the "feast," that is, the meeting for worship which
is held every nineteen days. He is also expected to con-
tribute to the Baha'i "fund," and to hold his own "firesides" for the purpose of converting others. Each month
he receives a copy of *Baha'i News*, which is "for circula-
tion among Baha'is only."

According to Baha'i reports, the "Nine Year Plan"
adopted in 1964 was most successful. In the U.S.A. the
number of registered members increased from seventeen
thousand in 1967 to twenty-two thousand in 1969, a third
of whom were said to be in California. *The American
Baha'i* of April, 1973, announced that the number of
Baha'is in the U.S.A. has tripled in the past ten years,
and that there are now members of the Faith in six thousand localities. Most of the members are young people
and people from minority groups. In a few weeks in the
winter of 1970-1971 thousands of black people in the
southern part of the U.S.A. were converted.

An announcement of the showing of a Baha'i film,
which tells the story of "more than 20,000 Americans in
South Carolina [who] have enrolled in the Baha'i Faith
since 1970," appeared in the *New York Times* of April 8,
1972. One who was interested to learn who these new

converts are, and how they were converted, made a journey to South Carolina, and reported as follows in a
letter to the editor of *The Christian Century*:

> I am currently writing a book about Baha'i in
> America and recently visited several of the "mass
> conversion" regions in South Carolina and Mary-
> land. The method of conversion: roving groups of
> visiting Baha'is went from house to house up and
> down the roads asking the rural blacks if they
> believed in peace, brotherhood and equality. When
> the response was "Yes" the blacks were told that in
> that case they were Baha'is and should sign the
> declaration cards to affirm their belief. They were
> not told about many of the restrictions which the
> Baha'i faith would place on them. . . . In some
> instances rural blacks were led to believe that edu-
> cational, scholarship and welfare programs would
> result from this membership in Baha'i.

In April and May of 1973 there was a general cele-
bration of the successful conclusion of the "Nine Year
International Teaching Plan," which had been "a period
of unprecedented growth of the worldwide Baha'i community."

Though reports indicate that the increase in membership has been great, there are indications that a considerable cooling off or even falling away of members
who were formerly quite active is occurring as well. It
is said that one reason for this is the authoritarian rule
of the present Administration. If some Baha'is thought
that by eliminating a Guardianship they would get more
freedom, they have been sadly disappointed. It is reported that members of the Faith spy on one another,
and live in fear of what might happen to them if they
are suspected of being disloyal to their rulers. It seems
that the Infallible Universal House of Justice of nine
members has inherited both the position and the spirit
of the Infallible Guardian, and no one dares to question its

authority. For example, all Baha'is were ordered to have no dealings with Mason Remey, who had been expelled, and not even to open letters from him. Of course, some believers like a dictatorship, whether it be a rule of one or of nine. But if this sort of rule continues, it is probable that there will be yet further losses.

What is the total number of Baha'is in the world? A leader of the Cause, speaking in a public meeting in New York in 1964, stated that the number was two million, but he did not indicate where all these believers were to be found. When asked how many Baha'is are now in Iran, one of the leaders in that land replied, "It is very difficult to give the number of adult Baha'is in Iran, because any figure we give you in Iran or any part of the world today is obsolete tomorrow with the Faith growing so rapidly." Likewise, all Baha'i publications and pronouncements give the impression that the growth of the movement is phenomenal, and that it is exercising a great influence in all parts of the world. Because of the vagueness of available statistics, the author sent a questionnaire to individuals in various countries, many of them in a position to know of any new religious movement. Replies were as follows:

From North Africa: "I have not come across a single Baha'i, foreign or native."

From Pakistan: "There were in 1969 more than 1,000 but not over 3,000 Baha'is, the majority of whom are of Iranian Muslim extraction, though some were formerly Hindus or Christians. Some of the leaders are well educated."

From Bangladesh: "There is one Baha'i couple from another country, but they have no knowledge of any indigenous Baha'i work in Bangladesh."

From Burma: "I do not recall having any contact with Baha'is in Burma, unless it had been an occasional

American traveler going through."

From the Philippines: "I have not seen any evidence of this religion until recently I came across a little ad in the Manila Times."

From Korea: "The Baha'i Cause was established in 1950 at the time of the Korean War by several American service-men and most of the Korean converts have been people from service-connected civilian or military groups or from universities. The Baha'is are beginning to try to make converts from the Christians in the churches. They claim a membership of 11,000, but probably have no more than 4,000 members, and do not seem to be increasing in numbers."

Letters sent to long-time residents in Japan, India, Yucatan, Indonesia, Lebanon, and other lands brought no reply, presumably because of a lack of information regarding the presence of Baha'is in those lands.

From Iran, however, two reliable informants who have for many years been in close touch with the Baha'i Cause, and whose near relatives are among the Baha'i leaders of that land, wrote full replies to the questionnaire. Among other things they said:

> The Baha'is do not have educational institutions. They have big firms and factories . . . and employ large numbers, perhaps many thousands. They mostly employ Baha'is. There are also many well-known doctors and specialists [who are Baha'is]. There are also many in high places in Government service. There are two to three hundred local groups of not more than a hundred each in Teheran, making a total of around 20,000.

No estimate was given as to the number in the provinces of Iran, but it is probably not greater than in the capital. While Baha'is are ready to conceal their faith when the situation requires it, many are proud to profess their faith openly. No Jews are now becoming Baha'is, "unless for personal benefits."

The Baha'i religion is not recognized by the government of Iran, but Baha'is are not persecuted by the government if they are good citizens, and the people of Iran do not generally oppose them. It is probable that some of the Baha'is in high positions have taken an important part in the recent reforms in Iran, but they did not do so as Baha'is. To the question, "How do average Baha'is compare with Muslims in Iran in moral character?" the correspondent replied that since they consider Baha'ism to be a "modern religion," they are less honest and moral than religious Muslims. "They think they are only required to believe in Baha'u'llah." To the question, "Will Iran ever become a Baha'i country?" the reply was "NEVER. It may become anything but Baha'i. . . . Baha'i laws are not practical for managing the Government."

One of the recent achievements of the Cause, of which Baha'is are rightly proud, and into which they have poured their contributions for many years, is the establishment of the Headquarters at Haifa and Akka (Acre) in Israel. The beautiful buildings and grounds in which the sacred shrines are located are visited annually by tens of thousands of tourists, both from Israel and from foreign lands, and the impression made on many of them is doubtless most favorable. The Baha'i leaders, shortly after the establishment of the State of Israel, declared that they would make no effort to convert the Jews to their religion, and it is said that they have kept their word. As a result, they have enjoyed the favor of the Israeli Government, and have recently received official recognition as one of Israel's religions. No doubt the tourists bring considerable income to the country. It is said that at the shrines Baha'i literature is given to visitors only when they ask for it.

In the time of Baha'u'llah and Abdu'l-Baha, the Baha'is in Akka and Haifa, who were mostly Iranians, lived and worshipped like the Sunnite Muslims about them, and the local population and officials considered them a sect of Islam. But since the increase of Western control in the Baha'i Faith, and especially since the establishment of Jewish rule in Palestine, it seems that little evidence of Islamic influence remains at the Baha'i Headquarters. If the Muslims, Christians, and Jews residing in that region of Israel knew what the Baha'is really believe, they might not be as friendly to them as they are said to be. But care is taken that they remain in ignorance. It seems rather strange that the Baha'i missionaries are attempting to convert all the people of the world, except those nearest to them in Israel.

13

Conclusion

ANY SYSTEM THAT CLAIMS to be a universal religion thereby invites the earnest consideration and careful appraisal of all who are seeking for God and for true life in this world and the next. The "Baha'i World Faith" is not just a crusade for world peace and unity and equity, important as these goals are. Rather, as has become clear in the preceding chapters, it claims to be the one true faith for the whole world for a thousand years, uniting in itself all previous religions and taking their place. As is stated in the Introduction to vol. XIII of *The Baha'i World,*

> It is the avowed faith of Baha'is that this Revelation has established upon earth the spiritual impulse and the definite principles necessary for social regeneration and the attainment of one true religion and social order throughout the world.

It is, therefore, our privilege and responsibility to carefully weigh the validity of this high claim.

Whoever peruses the thousands of pages of the thirteen large volumes of *The Baha'i World* will be impressed by the fact that the Baha'i Faith is indeed a world faith. For Baha'is, as well as for Christians and Muslims, "the field is the world," and it is their aim to bring the Good News of Baha'u'llah to all peoples, and

to unite all the conflicting religions in one. In a world
sorely divided, any effort to unite mankind in the bonds
of true brotherhood is to be commended. In order to
convert the people of the world to this Faith, Baha'is
have been most zealous in their missionary work. Believing that they have the latest and best religion in the
world, they use every means in their power to propagate
it, not only in their home communities, but also in foreign lands where, in obedience to the command of their
leaders, they have gone to reside. One cannot but admire
the zeal of those who, with heart and mind and hands,
work for a cause in which they believe.

Zeal, and even the readiness to die for a cause, do not
necessarily prove the cause's validity and value, however;
history reminds us that there have been many martyrs
who have died for error as well as for truth. Whether
the devoted missionaries are Mormons or Muslims, Bap-
tists or Baha'is, their message must be examined and
evaluated on its merits. What then shall we say of the
teachings of the Baha'i Faith as set forth in the writings
of Baha'u'llah and those who followed him? It would
seem that, in the official literature of the Faith, special
emphasis is placed on the Principles which were listed
and discussed in Chapter 10. Though the tabulation of
these Principles should be attributed to Abdu'l-Baha
rather than to his father, and though they are not original with him, certainly most persons of good will would
readily assent to the importance of "independent investigation of truth," "unity of mankind," "international
peace," "conformity of religion to science and reason"
(provided it is true science and sound reason), "banishment of all prejudice," "equality of men and women,"
"a world parliament," "universal education," and "a
universal language." These are social and ethical teachings which people of most religions, as well as people
of no religion, might adopt. They are not strictly reli-

gious principles, and there is no mention of God in connection with them.

To evaluate the Baha'i system as a religion, it is
necessary to go beyond the Principles to the laws of
Baha'u'llah which are contained in his *Kitab-i-Aqdas*,
summarized in Chapter 7. As the unprejudiced reader
peruses Baha'u'llah's regulations for worship in the Arabic language, for the nineteen-day fast, for the division
of inheritance, for the establishment of a nineteen-month
calendar with nineteen days in each month, for polyga-
mous marriages, and all the rest, how convinced is he
that this is the code of laws by which the lives of all
the people of the world should be regulated for the next
one thousand years? It has been said by some Baha'is
that the world is not yet ready to receive the laws of the
Kitab-i-Aqdas. This is no doubt true. But will it ever be
ready to adopt such a code?

Moreover, it is clear from the *Aqdas* and from the
writings of later leaders that the Baha'i Faith is political,
as well as social and religious, in its purpose and program. Baha'is look forward eagerly to the day when the
rulers of the nations will become believers and will use
their political power to support the Baha'i Faith and enforce its laws, when the Universal House of Justice will
become the Supreme Court of the World, and when not
only the personal lives of believers but also the political
affairs of the world will be ordered according to the laws
of Baha'u'llah. There is to be no separation of Church
and State in the Baha'i system. Prior to the death of
Shoghi Effendi in 1957, one of the chief merits of the
Faith, according to Baha'i writers, was the abiding presence in the world at all times of a living infallible leader
and guide, who would be the supreme head of the world
"Church-State." Since the First Guardian died without
appointing a successor, most of the Baha'is agree that
this rule now resides in the nine-member Universal
House of Justice, and infallibility is now claimed for this

body. It would indeed be a welcome and wonderful
change to live in a world whose rulers were infallible,
but such a hope was shattered by Baha'u'llah himself
when he stated in the *Aqdas* that infallibility belongs to
the Manifestation (Baha'u'llah) alone.

Since "the tree is known by its fruit," we may ask
how effectively Baha'is have practiced their Principles
and obeyed their Laws. It seems that their greatest success has been the absence of racial prejudice within
their community and their promotion of good race relations. As to this, the efforts of the Baha'is, both in the
U.S. and in other lands, are most commendable, and it
is not surprising that members of minority groups are
attracted to a movement that cordially accepts them. It
would seem that, in America and probably also in other
lands, the strongest appeal of the Faith is not so much
its teachings, but the fellowship which it offers, the
feeling of belonging to a community, something which
its converts had probably not found elsewhere. Since
local Baha'i units are usually not large, members are
drawn close together in the service of the Cause.

As for international peace, like many other groups,
religious and secular, Baha'is have talked much about
peace and have no doubt done what they could to achieve
the goal predicted by the ancient prophets of Israel and
announced by Baha'u'llah as the "Most Great Peace." In
addition to what individuals may have done in their
writings and addresses, *The Baha'i World*, vol. XIII, contains a proposal submitted by the Baha'i International
Community to the United Nations for a revision of its
Charter. This proposal includes a World Super-State to
which all nations would cede every claim to make war,
as well as many other powers. It also proposes an International Executive adequate to enforce supreme and un-
challenged authority on every recalcitrant member of
the Commonwealth, a World Parliament whose members
are elected by the people of their respective countries,

and a supreme Tribunal whose judgment would have a binding effect. If the United Nations considered this proposal at all, it does not seem to have viewed it with favor.

In education, medicine, and other fields, Baha'is in Iran and other lands have rendered valuable service, usually in a private capacity and not in the name of their Faith. In vol. XIII of *The Baha'i World*, which reports fully the activities of believers in all lands for the years 1954-1963, the reader found only one mention of a Baha'i service institution — a home for the aged in Wilmette.

On the other hand, Baha'is have not practiced the fine Principle designated "independent investigation of truth" with much vigor. One wonders how an open-minded Baha'i might investigate the history and doctrine of his religion while under the rule of an infallible Center of the Covenant, or Guardian, or House of Justice, which claim the sole authority to interpret the sacred writings. Such investigation is especially difficult since the *Kitab-i-Aqdas* is not yet available to Baha'is, who have been strictly forbidden to read a translation of the *Aqdas* by non-Baha'i scholars.

Important as the laws and ethical and social teachings of a religion are, its basic beliefs about God and man are of even greater importance since all else depends on them. What answer does it give to the questions which men have asked in all ages — Who or What is God? What is man? How can man know God? What must man do to be accepted by God? How can man be rid of the sin and evil which darken his life and separate him both from God and man? What does God want man to be and to do? Is there life after death? The value of any religion depends to a considerable degree on its ability to provide adequate answers to these and similar questions.

What does the Baha'i Faith tell us about God? Baha'-

u'llah taught that God is unknowable, except through
his Manifestations — Adam, Noah, Abraham, Moses,
Jesus, Muhammad, and Baha'u'llah — each Manifestation
more perfect than that preceding it. Baha'u'llah taught
that all the Manifestations are one, as today's sun is the
same as yesterday's. However, anyone who takes a close
and careful look at these "suns" will realize that they
differ greatly from one another, and it would seem that
God has changed his character as well as his laws on
each appearance, and not always for the better. When
Zoroaster, Buddha, and finally Krishna were later included as Manifestations, the confusion became com-
pounded. The Bab taught that there could be only one
sun in the heavens at a time to reveal the One God. But
if Zoroaster, Buddha, and Krishna are also Manifestations, there would have been two or more suns in the
sky at once, and it would seem that God had become
twins or triplets. Hence, the modern Baha'i message
about God is far from clear and by no means adequate.
Each believer probably brings to his Baha'i faith the
conception of God which he had from his previous faith,
or no-faith. The former Jews, Christians, and Muslims
would think of God as One, and former Hindus might
continue to believe in a multitude of gods. The reply of
the Baha'is would no doubt be that, in this age, God is
revealed more perfectly than ever before in Baha'u'llah.
We might inquire which of the divine attributes are revealed more perfectly in Baha'u'llah than in the great
prophets of the Old Testament, or in Jesus Christ, and
whether God's love is more perfectly manifested in
Baha'u'llah's service to the world than in the service of
any other messenger of God?

One of the phrases frequently found in Baha'i literature is "progressive revelation." It is said that people
usually think of prophets as men who lived and revealed
God in the distant past, and do not imagine it possible
for God to reveal himself now. "Yet Baha'u'llah not only

lived in our time, but was contemporary in the fullest
sense of the word. His teachings are . . . extremely advanced," says one Baha'i writer. We are compelled to
ask, "Is Baha'u'llah really contemporary?" He died in
1892. If it is God's plan, through "progressive revelation,"
to send new Manifestations to guide the people of the
world in new situations, surely the world today needs
something more relevant than the *Kitab-i-Aqdas*, and a
person closer to us than Baha'u'llah. But, according to
Baha'u'llah, no new Manifestation will come before 2866
A.D. If many of Baha'u'llah's pronouncements seem to
apply to our present situation, so do the Ten Commandments, and the Sermon on the Mount. A study of the
Aqdas will make it clear that Baha'u'llah is much closer
to the Middle Ages than to the twentieth century.

What is the Baha'i doctrine of man? Since, except
when Christians are being addressed, God is not usually
called "Father" in Baha'i teaching, man is not considered
a child of God, but his servant or slave. Nevertheless,
the Baha'i view of man is quite optimistic, for it teaches
that all man needs is laws, precepts, and an Educator.
The evil that resides in man's heart, be he savage or
civilized — evil that causes the horrible crimes which
blot the histories of the most "advanced" nations — is
largely ignored. Neither in the writings of the Bab, nor
in those of Baha'u'llah and the later leaders, except when
they are denouncing their enemies, is there any adequate
consideration of man's sin. There are few appeals to men
to repent of their sins as the prophets of old appealed,
and few assurances of God's love for sinners, or promises
of forgiveness and a new life of holiness.

Since the Baha'i diagnosis of man's condition is
faulty, its provision for man's salvation is inadequate. In
all Baha'i literature there is no promise of a Savior from
sin, or as appealing a picture of God welcoming a peni-
tent as the parable of the Prodigal Son. What hopeful
words would Abdu'l-Baha have said to a drug addict on

skid row, or to a convict in a death cell? Sinners need
salvation, and the Baha'i Faith fails to provide a Savior.

"If a man die shall he live again?" asked Job. Baha'-
u'llah's reply to this vital question is vague and unsatis-
fying. In the Baha'i system Resurrection means the
coming of a new Manifestation. Phrases such as "drinking the wine of immortality," "Paradise of Abha, the
everlasting abode of glorious, sacred souls," are found
in the *Adqas* and in other Baha'i writings. But it is not
clear whether they promise personal immortality or
merely the merging of man with the Infinite, like the
return of a rain drop to the sea from which it came.

For many students of Baha'i history, one of the Faith's
most disappointing aspects is the failure of its founders
and leaders to reveal, in their personal lives, or in their
dealings with members of their families and others who
differed with them, the spirit of love which they so
often spoke about, and which they enjoined on others.
Baha'u'llah's relations with his brother Subh-i-Azal,
Abdu'l-Baha's relations with his brother Mirza Muhammad Ali, and Shoghi Effendi's relations with numerous
relatives and former friends, revealed a bitterness that
was hardly a worthy example for their followers. We
are reminded of the question asked by another spiritual
teacher, "He that loveth not his brother whom he hath
seen, how can he love God whom he hath not seen?"
And how can he adequately and effectively manifest
God's love to others?

With the lack of clarity in its doctrine of God; with
the legalism which characterizes its Most Holy Book,
Kitab-i-Aqdas; with its prescription of practices long out-
dated; with the inadequacy of its treatment of sin and
of its provision for the cure of evil in man; with the
vagueness of its teaching about life after death; with the
gross failure of its founders to exemplify toward their
own families the love they so strongly advocated; and
with its utterly unrealistic plan for a religio-political

world government, the basic laws for which are contained in the *Kitab-i-Aqdas*—with these and other defects manifest in its history and in its teachings, can the Baha'i World Faith be an adequate religious and social system for the whole world of today and for the millennium to come? Only one answer is possible, and that is decidedly negative.

Where then shall one look for truth and love, for knowledge of God and hope for a better world? Only in the spotless life of Jesus Christ as it is portrayed in the Bible, in his loving service to men, in his voluntary death on the cross for sinners, and in his glorious resurrection from the dead on the third day, have the holiness, love, and power of God been once for all adequately manifested. Only Jesus Christ is the "image of the invisible God," the one true Manifestation of God. From his face alone has there shone forth in perfection "the light of the knowledge of the glory of God." Through faith in him sinful men may find forgiveness and peace with God and their fellowmen. Only as the people of the world submit to his spiritual rule in their personal lives, and with the guidance and power of the Holy Spirit obey his teachings in their social and political relationships, will men one day be able to live together in peace and love, and make life on earth what God wants it to be.